New-York Historical Society. Museum and Gallery of Art

Catalogue of the Museum and Gallery of art of the New-York Historical Society

New-York Historical Society. Museum and Gallery of Art

Catalogue of the Museum and Gallery of art of the New-York Historical Society

ISBN/EAN: 9783743304413

Manufactured in Europe, USA, Canada, Australia, Japa

Cover: Foto ©Thomas Meinert / pixelio.de

Manufactured and distributed by brebook publishing software
(www.brebook.com)

New-York Historical Society. Museum and Gallery of Art

Catalogue of the Museum and Gallery of art of the New-York Historical Society

CATALOGUE

OF THE

MUSEUM AND GALLERY OF ART

OF THE

New-York Historical Society.

1887.

NEW YORK:
PRINTED FOR THE SOCIETY.
M.DCCC.LXXXVII.

TROW'S
PRINTING AND BOOKBINDING COMPANY,
NEW YORK.

FFICERS OF THE SOCIETY, 1887.

PRESIDENT,

JOHN ALSOP KING.

FIRST VICE-PRESIDENT,

HAMILTON FISH.

SECOND VICE-PRESIDENT,

JOHN A. WEEKES.

FOREIGN CORRESPONDING SECRETARY,

WILLIAM M. EVARTS.

DOMESTIC CORRESPONDING SECRETARY,

EDWARD F. DE LANCEY.

RECORDING SECRETARY,

ANDREW WARNER.

TREASURER,

ROBERT SCHELL.

LIBRARIAN,

JACOB B. MOORE.

EXECUTIVE COMMITTEE.

FIRST CLASS—FOR ONE YEAR, ENDING 1888.

JOHN S. KENNEDY, WILLIAM DOWD,
GEORGE H. MOORE.

SECOND CLASS—FOR TWO YEARS, ENDING 1889.

JOHN A. WEEKES, WILLIAM LIBBEY,
JOHN W. C. LEVERIDGE.

THIRD CLASS—FOR THREE YEARS, ENDING 1890.

EDWARD F. DE LANCEY, WILLARD PARKER, M.D.
DANIEL PARISH, JR.

FOURTH CLASS—FOR FOUR YEARS, ENDING 1891.

BENJAMIN H. FIELD, ROBERT LENOX KENNEDY,

JOHN A. WEEKES, *Chairman.*
JACOB B. MOORE, *Secretary.*

[The President, Recording Secretary, Treasurer, and Librarian are members, *ex-officio*, of the Executive Committee.]

COMMITTEE ON THE FINE ARTS.

ANDREW WARNER, CEPHAS G. THOMPSON,
JOHN A. WEEKES, GEORGE H. MOORE,
DANIEL HUNTINGTON, HENRY C. STURGES.

DANIEL HUNTINGTON, *Chairman.*
ANDREW WARNER, *Secretary.*

[The President, Librarian, and Chairman of the Executive Committee are members, *ex-officio*, of the Committee on the Fine Arts.]

NOTICE.

This Catalogue describes the objects on exhibition in the Museum and Gallery of Art of the New York Historical Society. The Abbott Collection of Egyptian Antiquities, more particularly noticed in the preface and introduction which are reproduced in the following pages with Dr. Abbott's Catalogue, became the property of the Society, by the liberality of citizens of New York, in 1860. Together with the Lenox Collection of Nineveh Sculptures, they constitute a Department of Antiquities, which, when increased by the American collections now awaiting the space and means of arrangement, will bear comparison with the collections of Europe.

In 1856 the Society determined to enlarge and extend their Art Collections, and provide a public Gallery of Art in the City of New York. The Committee on the Fine Arts, then established as a part of the administration of the Society, entered upon the duties assigned them with active zeal, and have steadily and successfully pursued that design. The results are to be seen in the collection of which the present Catalogue gives only an imperfect and partial view. Eight hundred and one pictures are here described, besides other objects of art—probably the largest permanent collection yet exhibited on this continent.

This Gallery now embraces the entire collection of the New

York Gallery of Fine Arts, which was finally transferred to the custody of the Society in 1858. Any notice of this collection would be deficient which should fail to commemorate the name of LUMAN REED, whose taste, judgment, and generosity formed the nucleus of what may now be justly regarded as the foundation of a great Gallery of Art. The pictures collected by Mr. REED are designated in this catalogue as belonging to the Reed Collection. In this connection the Society was chiefly indebted to the liberality and cordial coöperation of one of their most valued members, who was himself the chief promoter of the original design of the New York Gallery, Mr. JONATHAN STURGES.

Subsequent additions to the collection in this department have been of the highest importance. The Society was indebted to the munificence of Mr. THOMAS J. BRYAN for the gift in 1867 of his noble collection, so well known as the Bryan Gallery of Christian Art, which was chiefly arranged and described under his own direction. During a subsequent visit to Europe, Mr. BRYAN continued his purchases, still further to enrich this gallery, and the zeal and enthusiasm to which the Society is deeply indebted were uninterrupted to the very last hours of his life. The splendid results of Mr. BRYAN's judicious taste and persevering liberality, thus dedicated to the public in the interest of Art, are alike honorable to him, to the Society, and the City. "New York is destined to owe a great debt of gratitude to Mr. BRYAN, which this generation will not leave wholly to their children to discharge."

In 1882, one hundred and fifty-eight paintings, designated in this Catalogue as the Durr Collection, and comprising the most meritorious works of art in the collection of a lamented associate, the late Mr. Louis Durr, of this city, were selected, as far as possible, to include the greatest variety of subjects and artists, and presented to the Society by his executors, in accordance with the terms expressed in his last will, the remainder being sold to provide a fund for the increase of the collection. In forming his gallery, Mr. Durr, the son of a noted antiquary and virtuoso of Carlsruhe, Germany, and himself a votary from boyhood to the study of the old schools of paintings, enjoyed, in addition to his own matured experience, the advantage, afforded by intimate friendship, of an access to the judgment of many eminent German connoisseurs and authorities in art. The Durr Collection is especially valuable to the Society in increasing the admirable facilities, offered to the historical student in the Bryan Collection, for tracing the development and progress of painting during the long and important period between the fourteenth and eighteenth centuries. It will be more and more appreciated as the knowledge of it is henceforth extended, as will the devotion which its lamented founder manifested in its formation, and his public spirit and munificence in dedicating it to the use and enjoyment of the community.

THE

ABBOTT COLLECTION

OF

EGYPTIAN ANTIQUITIES.

PREFACE.

Upon exhibiting this Collection, it may be necessary to state that I do not profess to be a savan, or a decipherer of hieroglyphics, but merely an amateur collector of such objects of antiquity as appeared to me illustrative of the religious and other customs of the ancient Egyptians, in whose country I have passed the last twenty years of my life. To occupy my leisure hours was necessary, and I found it an agreeable pastime to dive into the tombs of the ancients and rescue from the hands of the many pilferers such objects as appeared to me worthy of notice, and I think I may without fear of contradiction, assert that every article in this collection is of undoubted antiquity. I have spared neither time nor expense in my efforts to obtain the finest and most genuine objects of antiquity, and feel assured that they will be appreciated.

As regards the Catalogue, I have endeavoured, as far as the limits of such a work will allow, to give a sufficient, although not a very enlarged, description of each article, and for more minute details must refer to the works of such savans as Sir Gardner Wilkinson, S. Poole, Esq., I. Perring, Esq., J. Kenrick, Esq., Professor Lepsius, and M. E. Prisse, from all of which I have quoted when necessary.

Subjoined is an Introduction by a gentleman of this city, who has visited Egypt, and who is himself an author of great merit. He has rendered it useless for me to say more than that I am indebted to him and many other American travellers for the praise they have kindly bestowed upon my exertions, and without whose advice I should never have ventured to offer this Collection of Egyptian Antiquities to the patronage of the American public.

H. ABBOTT.

INTRODUCTION.

This Museum of Egyptian Antiquities was collected by Dr. Abbott, during a residence of twenty years in Cairo, all which time his attention was constantly directed to the subject. The most distinguished Egyptian scholars, Sir Gardner Wilkinson, I. Perring, Lepsius, and Poole, have verified in this collection many of their speculations, and the genuineness of the relics has, in their sanction, the highest possible authority. Many of the objects were found in tombs opened in the presence of Dr. Abbott, and there is probably no similar museum in the world more valuable to the Student, the Antiquarian, and the Divine. "There is nothing new under the sun," said Solomon, and here are many things that were old when he said it. It is here that the ocular and palpable evidence of the authenticity of the Bible is presented in the most interesting form. We are made, as it were, contemporary with Abraham, with the Israelites in Egypt, with Shishak, with Zerah, by witnessing specimens of rare arts made in their times, and with which they were familiar. Here, too, we must unlearn some of our pride, and be struck with new astonishment at the civilization of a people, whose historical records have mostly perished. The Biblical student will naturally turn in this Collection to the stone head of the Pharaoh of the Exodus, Thothmes III. of Egyptian history, which preserves the character of the Egyptian type, as seen in the Statues of Aboo Simbel, and in the face of the Sphynx—and which scientific research is unable to refer to one of the primeval races, so as to determine the probable origin of the Egyptians. He will also see the *iron* helmet and breast-plate of scale armour, bearing the cartouche, (corresponding to our modern armorial bearings,) of Shishak, nine hundred and seventy-one years before Christ, who took Jerusalem from Rehoboam.—2 *Chron.* xi. Also, a hawkheaded Vase, in green earthenware, from the plain of Zoan, with the oval of Zerah, the Ethiopian king, seven hundred and forty-one years B. C.—2 *Chron* xiv. Also the burned and unburned bricks made without straw by the children of Israel in Egypt, and dating from the above-mentioned Pharaoh. The Antiquarian will notice among a large collection of jewelry, the gold Necklace and Ear-rings bearing the name of Menes, the first Pharaoh of Egypt, and the earliest king in history. The most learned scholars assign two thousand seven hundred and seventy-one years B. C. as the date of these ornaments. The large gold Signet-ring of Shoofoo or Cheops, as High Priest and King; he was the builder of the great Pyramid two thousand three hundred and fifty-two years B. C. Baked clay stamps used by Terak, in the XXV. Dynasty, seven hundred and fourteen years B. C., to stamp the fresh Nile mud which was plastered over the locks of the granaries and the public buildings. Besides these, there is especial interest in the various cloths of those remote periods—in the preserved fruits and grains, threads, needles, and household implements of those who

> "Walked about, how strange a story!
> In Thebes' streets three thousand years ago."

The Mummy-case which was handed round at banquets to remind the guests of their mortality—the *Stylus* with which the Greeks wrote, and the tablets upon which they were used—the Painter's palette—the remarkably fine specimens of Papyrus, upon which the writing is still so legible—Glass, beautiful as the famous Venetian glass—the various images, talismans, and charms—the human Mummies, and three ponderous Mummied bullocks, all make real to the observer the daily life and habits of a people which, after centuries of supremacy, exists for him only in these relics.

THE

ABBOTT COLLECTION

OF

EGYPTIAN ANTIQUITIES.

---

1. A colossal Head in sandstone, the face painted red the colour the ancients always used to represent a native Egyptian. This fine head was brought from Thebes by I. Perring, Esq., and is a portion of a colossal statue of Thothmes III., who, according to Sir Gardner Wilkinson, was the Pharaoh of the Exodus, which event took place during his reign, in the month Epiphe, 1491 years before the birth of our Saviour. This Pharaoh is wearing the "ouabsh" or white crown of Upper Egypt, with the "uraeus" or sacred serpent, emblem of royalty, in front.

2. A shelf containing Earthenware Jars of the most elegant form. The large jar upon which the number is placed, was, when found, full of eggs; the others are supposed to have contained wine, and are pointed at the ends to enable them to be stuck in the sand.

3. A piece of Linen, inscribed, from a Theban Mummy.

4. Bricks of unburned clay, supposed to have been made by the Israelites, some bearing the stamp of their task-master, Thothmes III., and were found at Sakkarah, others were found at Heliopolis.

5. A piece of Linen Cloth in which a Mummy was enveloped. From Thebes.

6. A magnificent Vase of white marble, cut out of a solid piece. From Sakkarah.

7. A piece of Linen, a shroud. From Thebes.

8 A piece of Linen, inscribed,—the figure represents Amunoph 1st, a Pharaoh of the 18th Dynasty, 1550 years before Christ. From Thebes.

9. A piece of woollen Cloth worked in the corners. From Sakkarah.

10. A Shelf of Vases in common Earthenware, of various forms. From Sakkarah.

11. A most magnificently Carved Slab of Limestone, from the Temple of Erment. The hieroglyphics are most beautifully executed in relief. It represents the return of a king of the 13th Dynasty, or perhaps a more ancient Pharaoh on his return in triumph from a distant war, about 1850 years B. C.

12. A Figure of a Warrior in relief. From Lower Egypt.

13. An Inscribed Stone from a tomb. From Lower Egypt

14. A Limestone Slab covered with beautifully and deeply cut hieroglyphics. From a tomb in Sakkarah.

14½. A Fragment of Papyrus, supposed, from the style of the figures, to be of the Ptolemaic Period. From Abouseer

15. A piece of very fine Linen. From Thebes.

16. A piece of Linen, a shroud. From Thebes.

17. Six conical Stamps for securing the locks of public buildings or granaries; the locks were covered with the mud of the river Nile, and while wet were stamped with the government stamp, and of course could not be opened without breaking the seal.

18. A beautiful Earthenware Osirian Figure, with eleven lines of hieroglyphics. This figure is beautifully coloured, and is covered with a vitrous composition, and similar figures have rarely or ever been found. From Sakkarah.

19. A very beautiful Osirian Figure in white limestone. So called from being offerings to the god Osiris, from friends of the deceased, and are inscribed with a prayer for the deceased.

20. Another figure resembling No. 18, but having only nine lines of hieroglyphics; still these two figures appear to be moulded by the same hand, and the inscriptions are of the same import.

21. An Osirian figure in blue porcelain, having the car touche or oval of Psammetichus, who was a Pharaoh of the 26th Dynasty, 668 years B. C.

22. A very beautiful white limestone Osirian Figure, inscribed with six rows of hieroglyphics coloured with a blue pigment.

23. Twenty blue Porcelain Figures, covered with hieroglyphics from Colonel Campbell's tomb, near the great pyramid of Ghiseh.

24. A figure of a Female, in a recumbent position, of the Ptolemaic period. From Sakkarah.

25. A piece of Linen, painted with large hieroglyphical figures. From Sakkarah.

26. A piece of Woollen Cloth, striped brown and yellow.

27. A linen Shroud. From Dashour.

28. A piece of fine Linen, painted and gilded. From Sak karah.

29. A piece of Linen.

30. Linen from a mummy of a military man, and has on the front the badge of his rank worked in black worsted. From Luxor.

31. A piece of Linen, inscribed with a line of hieroglyphics which appear to have been burnt in. From Sakkarah.

32. A fine piece of Linen, having the outline of Thoth, the Ibis-headed God, drawn upon it. From Sakkarah.

33. Woollen Cloth, yellow ground. with brown stripe From Sakkarah.

34. A piece of Fringed Linen. From Sakkarah.

35. The outline of a man having a crocodile on each side of him, drawn on a very fine piece of linen.

36. Pieces of very fine Linen, inscribed with the Ritual. From Sakkarah.

37. A Woollen Dress for a child, embroidered on the skirt and sleeves. From Sakkarah.

38. A piece of fine Linen. From Sakkarah.

39 A striped linen Scarf found in the cat-mummy pits at Sakkarah.

40. Thirteen earthenware Jars of various forms, the most curious of which is one in the form of a Fish.

41. A very old piece of Woollen Garment figured with red, blue, and yellow. From Dashour

42. Two common earthenware fire Blowers. From Sakkarah.

43. A small Coffin, in unbaked clay. From Thebes.

"At the entertainments of the rich, just as the company was about to rise from the repast, a small coffin is carried round, containing a perfect representation of a dead body, and the bearer exclaims,—'Cast your eyes on this figure, after death you yourself will resemble it—drink then and be happy.'"—*Vide Herodotus: Euterpe* LXXVIII.

44. A Brick with a cartouche of Thothmes III. From Thebes.

45. A Brick with the maker's stamp. From the city of On or Heliopolis.

46. An unbaked Brick. From the city of On.

47. A marble Statue in the sitting posture, sculptured on the sides and having a cartouche of royalty. From Sakkarah.

48. The portrait of a Queen, in sandstone. From the temple of Philæ.

49. A small stone Sarcophagus, containing the figure of the deceased, also in stone, inscribed, used for the same purpose as No. 43.

50. A stone Cone, found in the great pyramid of Cheops at Ghiseh.

51. A very magnificent funereal Papyrus, twenty-three feet long, containing the ritual of the dead in the Hieratic characters; it is illustrated with figures in outline. From Sakkarah.

52. The lid of the Sarcophagus, No. 49.

53. Stone Wedge, found in the pyramid of Cheops.

54. A stone Mallet, found with the above and with No. 50 at Ghiseh.

55 A portrait of a Queen, in sandstone. From the temple of Philæ.

56. A wooden figure of a Lion, inscribed down the breast —very ancient.

57. Fragment, in red granite, of the left foot of a statue of the great Rameses II. It is of colossal proportion; was found at Thebes. Rameses II. commenced his reign 1355 years B. C.

58. A small earthenware Bottle.

59. A small figure in sandstone, inscribed with a line of hieroglyphics down the middle. From Tourah.— *Vide Colonel Vyses' Work on the Pyramids.*

60. An Imitation of the head of a Mummy, in papier maché. From Sakkarah.

61. A fragment of a Papyrus, partially destroyed by fire, in the original linen wrapping. From Dashour.

62. A fragment of wooden Sarcophagus, painted.

63. A piece of Cord made from the fibre of the date-tree. From Dashour.

64. A curious Necklace of ivory. From Ghiseh.

65. A piece of a Papyrus, in the Greek characters, unrolled. From Sakkarah.

66. A Roll of Papyrus. From Thebes.

67. A marble Vase. From Sakkarah.

68. Coloured Binding. From Dashour.

69. White Binding. From Dashour.

70. An alabaster Vase, containing an unguent.

71. A fragment of Papyrus, wrapped in fine linen. From Thebes.

72. A vase of fine Clay, with a grotesque face. From Sakkarah.

73. A piece of Muslin, with a hawk painted upon it. From Ghiseh.

74. Ancient Cord from the bull pits of Dashour.

75. An alabaster Vase, similar to No. 70.

76. An earthen Jar, stained, to imitate red granite, and inscribed with one line of hieroglyphics. From Thebes. Also, two small pieces of painted cloth.

77. An earthenware Pitcher, ornamented with a brown pattern. From Lower Egypt.

78. A Jar similar to No. 76. From Thebes.

79. A Mummied Cat, in a carton case, inscribed with hieroglyphics. From the Cat-Tomb at Sakkarah.

80. A similar Vase to No. 72. From Sakkarah.

81. An earthenware Vase. Do. do.

82. An earthenware Vase. Do. do.

83. A very plain but highly interesting hawk-headed Vase, in blue porcelain, found in the plain of Zoan, inscribed with the name of Osorkon, the Ethiopian King, Zerah of the Scriptures, who reigned 945 years B. C., and who fought the battle with Asa, one of the Shepherd Kings, 941 years B. C.—*See II. Chron. Chap. XIV.*

84. A blue porcelain Figure, without a head, in a kneeling posture, inscribed down the back with hieroglyphics. From Ghiseh.

85. A miniature Bull's Head. From Sakkarah.

86. A Mummy Cat. From Sakkarah.

87. A Mummy Cat. Do. do.

88. An Arm of a wooden statue. From Ghiseh.

89. Two Cups, in white metal. From Tel-el-Yahoudi.

90. 

A Statue, of small size, in basaltic stone, of a Man, in that singular sitting posture, peculiar to Egypt; a line of well-cut hieroglyphics encircles the plinth, and a sentence is cut on the front of his dress. From Thebes.

91. A small Statue in limestone, of a Man, in the sitting posture, with a roll of Papyrus unrolled before him. From Thebes.

92 A Statue, in hard limestone, of a Man, in the attitude of prayer, admirably executed; some lines of hieroglyphics are sculptured on the front of his dress. From Thebes.

93. A figure of a Serpent, with a human head, in sandstone. From Sakkarah.

94. A small tablet representing the God Thoth, introducing the deceased to Phre, who is in the costume of Osiris. This tablet is curious from the circumstance of Thoth being of the same colour (blue) as the great divinity of Thebes.

95. A small tablet representing an Egyptian Lady in the attitude of prayer, making an offering to Phre, who is in the position and habit of Ammon, of whom also he has the azure complexion. From Thebes.

96. The name (or cartouche) of the great Rameses. From the tomb of the Kings in Thebes.

97. A small tablet of the same subject as No. 94, except that Phre in this tablet is accompanied by Isis and Nepthys. From Thebes.

98. A Vase of black Basalt. From Sakkarah.

99. An alabaster Vase.

100. A small Marble Vase.

101. An earthenware cooking Pot.

102. A small Vase, in green basalt.

103. A small Vessel, in limestone. From Tourah.

104. A small black marble Saucer, on which is the preparation used in embalming Mummies of the first class. Taken from a Mummy by Doctor Abbott. From Thebes.

105 A fish's Head, in earthenware. From Sakkarah.

106. A Figure of Typhon, in soft limestone. From Sakkarah.

107. A blue earthenware Necklace. Taken from a Colossal Statue at Sakkarah.

108. A mummied Ibis, in its original wrappings. From Sakkarah.

109. A mummied Hawk. From Sakkarah.

110 A mummied Ibis. From Thebes.

111. do. do.

112. The same as 108. Also, a lobster's claw.

113. Packages yet unwrapped.

114. Conical Stamps, with the name of Terak, Tirhakah of the Scriptures, 714 years B. C.

115. A Statue, in limestone, of a Man, sitting on a throne and wearing the projecting kilt; on each side of the seat is sculptured in low relief two men bearing offerings. From a tomb in Sakkarah

116. A limestone Slab, inscribed. From Sakkarah.

117. A Fragment, in limestone, of a person making an offering. From Sakkarah.

118. Limestone Slab, representing an offering to the God Osiris. The figures in this stone are curiously painted. From Thebes.

119. A Tablet, in sandstone, representing an offering; is valuable for the inscription. From Sakkarah.

120. A limestone Slab, representing a Man kneeling before an altar. From Sakkarah.

121. A Figure kneeling before the Deity and making an offering.

122. A very interesting Monument, having three cartouches; one over the fourth figure has been intentionally obliterated, of Amunoph and his family receiving homage. From Thebes.

123. A limestone Tablet, representing several figures making submission; very coarsely executed. From Sakkarah.

124. A finely executed Hawk, cut in hard limestone. This is one of the sacred birds of the Egyptians. From Sakkarah.

125. A fragment of an Altar, in sandstone, inscribed on each side. From Sakkarah.

126. Fragment of an Altar, in flinty limestone, bearing several ovals or royal names: it has some peculiarities in the hieroglyphics. From Sakkarah.

127. A figure in limestone, of a Man in a sitting posture The figure is painted a red colour, and wears a white cloth round his loins From Sakkarah.

128. A Fragment in basaltic stone, inscribed. From Sakkarah.

129 A fragment of a statue in black granite, of a Man bearing a kid on his shoulders. This fragment is of Græco-Egyptian art, and came from Lower Egypt.

130 A statue in limestone of a Priest, having on his knees an open volume of Papyrus which he appears to be reading; two lines of hieroglyphics encircle the plinth, with an additional line on the front, and the papyrus is inscribed with six rows of perpendicular hieroglyphics. From Thebes.

131. A fragment of a well-executed Figure, in basalt. From Thebes.

132. A statue of a Sphinx trampling upon a Serpent; it is of later times and involves some curious mythological mystery. From Sakkarah

133. A fragment of a Statue in limestone; a figure in a sitting posture, reading a Papyrus containing six lines of beautifully executed hieroglyphics; there is also a line of hieroglyphics on the plinth. From Ghiseh.

134. A fragment of a limestone Slab, of the time of Amunoph I., representing a man making an offering to that Pharaoh, who is seated and dressed as Osiris. From Sakkarah.

135. A small sandstone representation of an Entrance into a Tomb. From Sakkarah.

136. A Tablet in limestone. From Sakkarah.

137. A sandstone Tablet, broken. Do.

138. A Mummy of a child, with a gilded mask. From Sakkarah.

139. Five Jars, with the heads of the four Genii of Amenti.

These genii, as they are called, are variously represented, sometimes in the form of mummies, sometimes like the short vases here seen, in which the different viscera are supposed to have been preserved embalmed.

Each has a different head; one with a human head, called Amset, held the stomach and large intestines.

Hapi, with the head of a cynocephalus, the small intestines.

Smautf, or Lioutmouf, the lungs and heart.

Hebhsnauf, the liver and gall-bladder.—*Vide Kenrick.*

140. Three wooden Cats, with glass eyes, one has the face gilded—this contains the Mummy of a Cat. From the Cat Tombs of Sakkarah.

"The Cat was usually consecrated to the Moon: two reasons were assigned,—the first, that this animal brings forth one, then two and so on to seven in the whole twenty-eight, the number of the days of a lunation. This, PLUTARCH himself thought to border on the fabulous; of the second he seems to have judged more favourably—that the pupils of the cat's eyes are round at the full moon, but grow contracted and dull as she wanes."—*Ibid*, p. 17, Vol. II.

141. A white box, inscribed with the name of Amunoph IV., 1350 years B. C.; it originally belonged to a scribe. From Thebes.

142. Wooden Boxes found in a tomb at Ghiseh.

143. A fragment of Limestone, with figures. From Sakkarah.

144. A piece of Limestone, inscribed, and having the cartouches of Rameses IV., 1959 years before Christ. Found at Heliopolis.

145. Fragment of Sandstone, representing one of the Roman Emperors making offerings after the fashion of the Pharaohs to the Goddess of Truth, who is represented with an ostrich feather in her hand. The figures are in cavo relief, and the fragment was brought from Nubia.

146. The top of a Sarcophagus, made of burned clay, found in a tomb near Gebel Silsilis.

147. A kneeling Figure, in black basalt, holding before her a tablet inscribed with hieroglyphics. From Sakkarah.

148. Part of a lid of a Sarcophagus, in earthenware, painted,—was found at Tourah, where the Israelites were said to have been kept at work, and where there is an ancient Jewish cemetery.

149. A sitting Figure in black basalt, inscribed. From Sakkarah.

150. Another lid of a Sarcophagus, found with No. 146.

These are rare; indeed, are the only specimens I have met with.

151. Fragment, consisting of four pieces of limestone, being a portion of the false door-way always found in tombs, to render the real entrance to the inner room in which the bodies were generally placed, more difficult to be found. Taken from the tomb of a

priest in the time of Pharaoh Shapre. The hieroglyphics are in the style of the monuments about the Pyramid of Ghiseh, from which ancient city it was taken. Dashour.

152. Three large Mummies of the Sacred Bull, Apis, found in the Tombs at Dashour. These Mummies are very

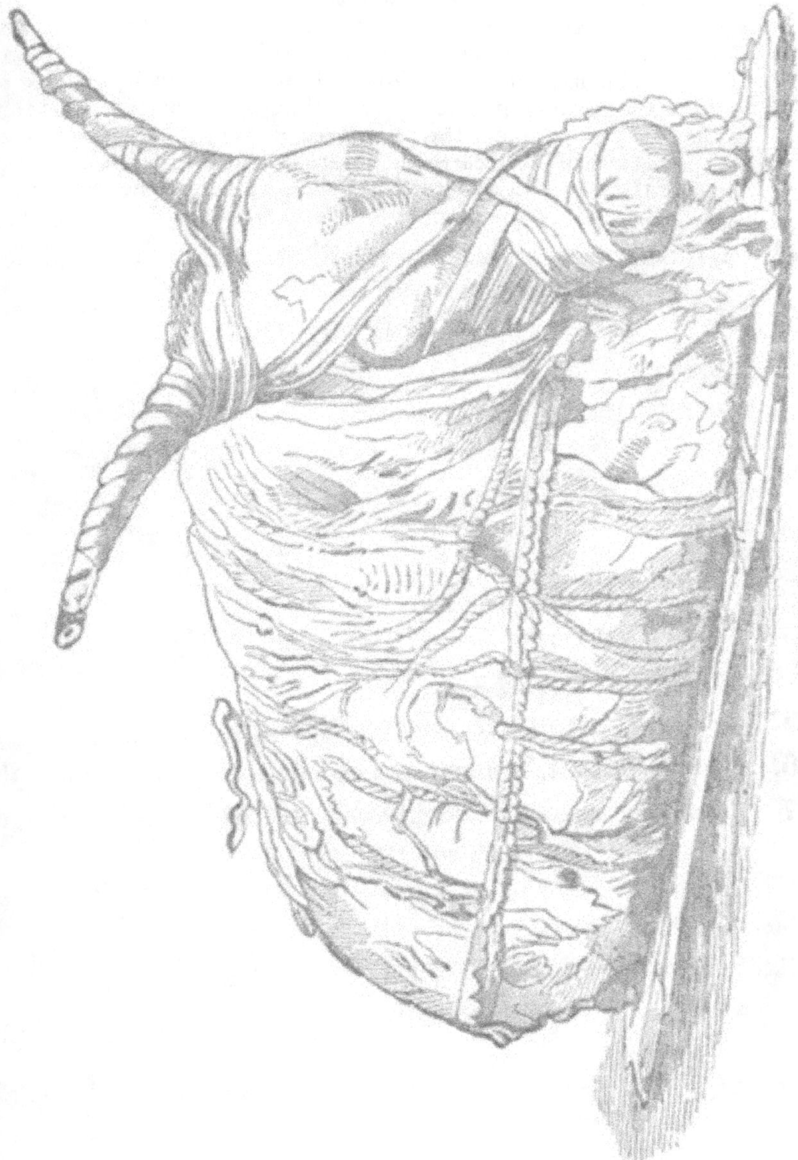

MUMMIED BULL.

rare—no other Museum possessing a single specimen.

"The Egyptians honoured him as an Image of the Soul of Osiris, and that this soul was supposed to migrate from one Apis to another, in succession. His death was a season of general mourning, and his interment was accompanied with the most costly ceremonies." *Vide Kenrick*,—p. 20, Vol. II.

In the same case will be found two skulls of the Sacred Bull, one with its horns crooked; there are also different bones, the largest of which are the vertebræ of the neck, which are of extraordinary size. On the back of the middle bull may be seen a net of rope used for the purpose of carrying any thing between two persons, a stick being passed under the two pieces of wood and supported on the shoulders of the carriers, together with a large rope-bag, found in the pits with the Bulls, supposed to be used to carry their food.

152½. A piece of ancient Rope. Brought from the Tombs at Dashour, by Dr. Abbott.

153. A small wooden Footstool. From Sakkarah.

154. A very handsome bronze Column mounted on a tripod terminating in lion's claws.

On the summit is a circular plate supporting a bronze vase, supposed to be used for burning incense or other offerings. This interesting object was found at Tel-el-Yahoudi, or the mound of the Jews, where, upon the site of an ancient Egyptian city, the Israelites were permitted by Ptolemy Philomater, upon the application of their High Priest, Onius, to build a temple. The place then became the resort of the Jews, and was called the City of Onion, or *Onii—Metropolis*, and was probably one of the five cities in the land of Egypt, which, according to Isaiah, "were to speak the language of Canaan."—*Vide Isaiah* XIX. 18.

155. A small Campstool. From Sakkarah.

156. A long Slab of Limestone inscribed. From Sakkarah.

157. The Figure of a humpback of the Ptolemaic age. From Heliopolis, the city of On.

158. Four wooden Cats, similar to No. 140.

159. Vases of Amenti.

160. The mummy of a Dwarf. From Sakkarah.

161. A small Altar stone with two hollow basins. From Tourah.

162. An Altar stone with a hollow depression, inscribed all around with hieroglyphics. From Sakkarah.

163. An Altar stone with one depression or hollow, inscribed all around the margin. From Sakkarah.

164. A similar Stone, likewise inscribed.

165. A large Stone of the same form inscribed.

166. A Stone similar to, but larger than No. 162.

167. A marble Statue, unfortunately imperfect, of a keeper of volumes, an officer of high rank, on each side of the pedestal is an inscription of hieroglyphics of very early style, and on the front are offerings most beautifully carved. From Sakkarah.

168. A Lion, from the neighbourhood of the Pyramids of Ghiseh.

169. A limestone representing some religious ceremony. From Sakkarah.

170. 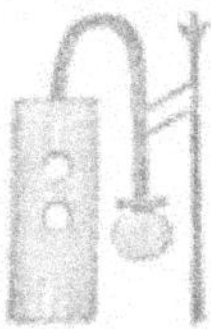 A Statue in limestone, of an Hierogrammatist, sitting and exhibiting a volume or Papyrus, on his knees.

This Statue is in good preservation, and is remarkable for the instrument which is hung over his left shoulder, representing a bag or basket, which the scribes carried with them, and hence used in the inscriptions as the symbol of that office and of the art of writing. From Thebes.

171. A Statue similar to No. 127.

172. An Altar-Stone for libations, very curiously carved and inscribed. From Lower Egypt.

173. Fragment of the Statue of an Egyptian Lady sitting on a stool.

In the line of hieroglyphics down the front of her dress, will probably be found the names of her parents. This fragment is of elegant design, and from the style about the time of Rameses. From Sakkarah.

174. Representation, in fine sand-stone, of a false door to a tomb having a Greek inscription. From Sakkarah.

175. A Broken Tablet, in sand-stone, the hieroglyphics in relief.

176. A small votive Tablet in low relief. From Sakkarah.

177. A very beautiful Tablet in limestone, of a man making offerings to Osiris. From Sakkarah.

178. A sand-stone Tablet, the figures in relief. From Sakkarah.

179. A limestone Tablet representing Amunoph the First making an offering to Osiris. From Sakkarah.

180. A Fragment in sand-stone defaced.

181. Fragment, representing art cles of food placed on a table. From a tomb in Sakkarah.

182. 183. Two conical Altars in limestone, with a similar inscription on each; and with a tazza in granite, also inscribed.

184. Group of figures about two feet high in fine limestone, from the quarries of Tourah.

It represents a man in an ancient dress and position, the left leg slightly advanced; his son sustaining his right knee, while his daughter, in a kneeling position, supports his left. This group still preserves much of its ancient colour. Such groups are common, in basso relievo, on the walls of the more ancient tombs. This is from the same tomb as No. 115, and Nos. 181, 182, 183.

185. Specimens of the Mummied Ibis found in earthenware pots, in the Ibis pits at Sakkarah.

186. A pair of Sandals belonging to a lady, made of the date leaf. From Dashour.

187. A Sandal, made of date leaf. From Sakkarah.

188. Ditto, do.

189. A Sandal beautifully made of the bark of papyrus.

190. Ditto, do.

191. A pair of curiously made Sandals for a lady.

192. Two feet beautifully executed in wood, from a coffin of a Mummy. From Ghiseh. These, though not finely finished, show the work of a master hand. The width between the great and second toes is the space occupied by the strap of the sandal.

193. Two beautifully preserved and magnificently wrapped specimens of the Ibis Mummies, found in the tombs of Sakkarah.

194. A very ancient Sandal from Ghiseh.

195. Ditto, do.

196. A Sandal made of the raw hide. From Ghiseh.

197. A pair of very elegantly made Sandals for a lady.

198. A pair of very handsome Sandals, coloured red.

199. A pair of purple leather Boots for a lady. From Dashour.

200. A pair of white Kid Boots.

201. A pair of very small leather Sandals for an infant.

202. A Child's leather Shoe.
203. A red leather Boot.
204. A specimen of Needlework. From Ghiseh.
205. Ditto, do.
206. A fine specimen of Linen Cloth.
207. A fine specimen of Woollen Cloth.
208. A specimen of Knitting in variously-coloured worsted
209. 210. 211. Knives of the Ethiopian Stone, used in making the incisions in the cavity of the abdomen in the process of embalming, the use of a metal instrument not being allowed.

Vide Herodotus, Euterpe, LXXXVI.

212. A skull of a female Mummy with plaited hair. From Sakkarah.
213. A skull of a female Mummy dressed with a cap of worsted work.
214. A skull of a Male Mummy with hair.
215. The leg of a Female wanting the foot, which had been amputated at the ankle-joint during life, prior to the process of embalming, as the cloth covers the articulating surface of the joint. From Sakkarah.
216. 217. Two Mummied Hands, gilded, from Ghiseh.
218. 219. Two Mummied Feet, gilded, from the same Mummy as the hands.
220. The hand of a Female Mummy, beautifully enveloped in cloth, from Sakkarah.
221. A Sandal from a Female Mummy, painted and gilded.
222. Four Mummied Ibises, from the pit at Sakkarah.
223. A pair of Sandals of raw hide, from Sakkarah.
224. A pair of Leather Sandals.
225. Three Mummied Hands. From Sakkarah.
226. A Sandal of date leaves, with the toe turned up and the sides raised, approaching the shape of a shoe. From Ghiseh.
227. A pair of Sandals, (right and left,) very neatly made, for a lady. From Dashour.

228. A round basket made of grass, having five partitions round a centre, in one of the partitions is No. 229

229. A white Glass, of beautiful form. From Sakkarah.

230. An ancient Broom made of straw, similar to those in use at the present day.

230½. A rude Scarabæus in wood, containing a mummied beetle. From Sakkarah.

231. A small figure of the Bull Apis. From Dashour.

232. A fragment of a Vase, covered with figures of the Persian period. From Ghiseh.

232. A Basket and Lid covered with red leather. The basket is made of fine reeds, and is divided into seven partitions. From Sakkarah.

234. A most magnificent Papyrus in the Hieratic character. thirty-six feet long, and in such perfect preservation that it does not require to be stretched on paper, Such Papyri are scarcely ever met with. This was found at Sakkarah.

235. The figure of a Goddess painted on cloth.

236. A pair of Sandals, covering the sides of the feet, made of date leaves. From Sakkarah.

237. A pair of purple Leather Boots, ornamented with gilded devices. From Sakkarah.

238. A pair of very curiously made Sandals for a Lady. From Sakkarah.

239. A Man's Sandal made of Papyrus leaves, turned up at the toes. Worn only by persons of rank.

240. A pair of red Leather Boots. Ditto.

241. A Man's Sandal of Papyrus leaves, turned up at the toe. From Thebes.

242. A pair of Leather Boots. From Abouseer.

243. A pair of do. very old, and in bad condition. Do.

244. A neatly made pair of Lady's Sandals.

245. A piece of the covering of a Mummy, with the figure of an Israelite bound and placed on the sole of a sandal as a mark of contempt. From Thebes.

246. A fragment of a Wooden Coffin, inscribed, and having two figures of Anubis (Jackals) watching. From Sakkarah.

247. Fragment of a Sarcophagus, with the figure of Nephthys. From Thebes.

248. A round Piece of Wood from the pyramid of Sakkaráh.

249. A small Piece of Wood from a wall in the entrance of the great pyramid at Abouseer.

250. A fragment of Granite of the god Nilus, inscribed. From Sakkarah.

251. A part of a Lyre in the shape of a swan's head, inlaid with ivory. From Sakkarah.

252. }
253. } Sacred Serpents with the disk originally gilded.

254. The head of a Duck in wood, most beautifully executed, in a miniature form. From Sakkarah.

255. A beautiful Figure in Wood, inscribed down the middle, and having the cartouche of Thothmes III., and the same royal name is on the banner held in his hand. From Thebes.

256. Lion's Head in wood, of excellent workmanship, which formed part of an elegant chair similar to those represented in the Baban el Molook. In one eye is still the remains of the gold orb and blue enamel of the lid. From Sakkarah.

257. Part of the arm of a Chair, inlaid with ivory, to represent a duck or goose's head. From Thebes.

258. A piece of a Tree taken from the wall in the chamber of the Great Pyramid of Sakkarah.

259. A leg of a Chair, inscribed. From Thebes.

260. A leg of a Chair, in hard wood, inscribed, and has the cartouche of Bukhan-a-ten-ra, a Pharaoh of the eighteenth dynasty; 1430 years before Christ.

261. A small figure of a Humpbacked Man in wood.

262. A Monkey seated on a Lotus.

263. Ditto. Ditto.

264. Cupping Horn, similar to those used in the East at the present time. The operator exhausts the air through a small hole at the point of the horn to which he applies his mouth, and then covers it with a small piece of leather which is attached to it for that purpose. It was found by Dr. Abbot in a tomb at Sakkarah, at the opening of which he was present.

265. A Cupping Horn, terminating in the head of a buffalo. From Sakkarah.

266. A Cupping Horn, terminating in the head of a lion.

267. Small Figure in hard brown wood, representing one of the Asiatic tribes prostrate. It probably formed part of a group, representing the king trampling under foot the enemies of Egypt. From Sakkarah.

268. Legs of an Ox, in wood, worn as a charm.

269. A Tablet in Wood, dedicated to Ammon, for the cure of deafness. From Thebes.

270. A Wooden Figure, similar to No. 267, the head curiously twisted to appear as if looking round.

271. A Figure of a Monkey, beautifully executed, but very old. From Abouseer.

272. A Sphinx, in wood.

273. An instrument in wood used by the Egyptian Priests in making offerings to their Gods. One end terminating in a hawk's head, the other in a hand. Very ancient. From Sakkarah.

274. A piece of Wood originally beautifully inscribed. From Sakkarah.

275. Statue of a Cynocephalus sitting; this animal is the symbolic hieroglyphic of the God Thoth, he is carved in stone and of good workmanship; there are a few hieroglyphics on the plinths in which the name of Thoth appears. From Lower Egypt.

276. A Cynocephalus in stone.
277. Ditto in earthenware.
} From Abouseer.

278.
279.
280.
} Osirian Figures in Wood, painted and inscribed From Thebes.

281. Statue of Isis and Horus in black stone; this figure has a legend in hieroglyphics on the plinth. From Sakkarah.

282. An Osirian figure in wood.

283. Statue of a King in stone holding the flagellum in his right hand, and the pastoral crook of Osiris in his left; he wears the projecting kilt, down the centre of which are two lines of hieroglyphics; the cap of the statue was of bronze, as appears from a portion still remaining. From Lower Egypt.

284. A Lamp in green porcelain, found in the great pyramid of Cheops at Ghiseh.

285. A similar Lamp found in the great pyramid of Sakkarah.

286. A circular lamp with two burners, with a socket in the centre to fix it on a staff. From Abouseer.

The ten accompanying lamps are of the Ptolemaic and early Christian period.

287. Small Statue in fine limestone, representing a person kneading dough or grinding.

This little figure is of admirable workmanship, and is inscribed with several lines of hieroglyphics which have been filled with some brilliant blue composition. The subject is not common. There are one or two examples of kings habited in the attire of a priest, and employed in the same occupation. From Thebes.

288. Statues of Isis and Horus, in white marble.

The Goddess has a bronzehead-dress, and a bronze hawk stands behind her throne, which it encircles with its extended wings. These were formerly beautifully inlaid with enamel or some other vitrous substance, but age has nearly destroyed all traces of it. The plinth of this curious and rare specimen is of bronze, and there is an inscription in hieroglyphics down the back of the Goddess. From Sakkarah.

289. 290. } Two green glass Bottles found in a tomb at Sakkarah.

291. A porcelain figure of a Female in a white dress, and her head decorated with the lotus flower and leaf, intermixed with gold, showing the style of dress of her time, Thothmes III. From Thebes.

"It was probably used as a pattern."—Vide Herodotus, Euterpe, lxxxvi.

292 A figure of Bacchus bearing a Wine Jar, beautifully executed in earthenware. From Lower Egypt.

293. } Figures of the God Onouris, emblematical of Evil
294. } and Death. From Sakkarah.

295. A small earthenware Vase of an antique form. From Sakkarah.

296. Figure of a Female of the Ptolemaic period, in red earthenware. From Abouseer.

297. A Vase in the form of a Female holding a gazelle on her left arm; this Vase is made of fine red clay. From Sakkarah.

298. A similar figure to No. 293, having a serpent in each hand in place of the shield and sword. From Sakkarah.

299. A Figure of a Horus in red clay, of the Ptolemaic time. From Sakkarah.

300. The Figure of RA. or the Sun. on a lotus leaf. From Ghiseh.

301. A figure of a Monkey, in red clay.

302. A Comic Mask, in red clay.

303. Part of a Mould in soft stone for casting various devices. It is of the Ptolemaic age; for, on one side is the head of Jupiter Serapis. From Sakkarah.

304. A Series of 12 Moulds for casting. The one numbered is a mould of the god Pthah Socharis, the divinity of Memphis. From Sakkarah.

305. A Head in burned clay. Apparently of an idiot.

306. A Figure, similar to 294.

307. Model of a Hoe, in limestone.

308. The figure of a man of the lower class, in brick.

309. A model in porcelain, of the Staff held by the deities of Egypt, from which it will be seen, that the upper termination of these staves is not intended to represent the Hoopoo or any other bird, but that of some quadruped with long ears. Found at Sakkarah.

310. } Two Osirian Figures, both broken but inscribed, and
311. } have the cartouche of Psammetichus.

312. A Porcelain Cylinder, inscribed. From Ghiseh.

313. Figure of the God Nilus, in white marble.

314. A Cow's head, in porcelain.

315. A mass of Osirian figures, that have been spoiled and rejected by the manufacturers. From Thebes.

316. A porcelain representation of the Pandean Pipes From Sakkarah.

317. A Wooden Figure of Osiris, beautifully covered with gold leaf.

318. A Wooden Figure of the Goddess Isis and her son Horus. From Sakkarah.

318½. A Stone Stamp with a royal name (cartouche) on it.

319. A Basket, the lid is ornamented with shells. From Sakkarah.

320. A Figure of Horus and Isis, in its original wrapping.

321. A Figure of Osiris, in its original wrapping.

322. A small Basket found in one of the chambers of the Great Pyramid at Sakkarah, by I. Perring, Esq.

323.
324.
325. Three small coarse Baskets made of the fibre of the date tree.

They were deposited with the Mummy, and intended to contain the grain which it was supposed the deceased would require in the cultivation of the fields of Amenti, during his progress in the lower hemisphere or purgatory. See any of the funereal Papyri and also the small Osirian figures. One of these baskets is almost invariably represented slung over the left shoulder of the blue figures by a cord held in the right hand, together with an instrument representing the hoe, while in the left hand is another instrument of agriculture. These baskets are by no means common, and are found only in a certain class of Mummy. From Thebes.

326 A piece of thin Cord, beautifully made and in good preservation. From Abouseer.

327. A piece of Cord, made from the fibre of the date tree.

328. An ingeniously constructed trap for catching the Gazelle.

It is made of the points of the date leaves, so arranged as to entangle the animal's leg when trodden upon, and to prevent him from running, while the hunters are enabled to come up and catch him. From Sakkarah.

329. An ancient Basket. From Thebes.

330. A piece of a Mummy case, inscribed, and bearing a cartouche upon it. From Sakkarah.

331. A gilded figure of Osiris holding a bronze crook in his left hand. From Sakkarah.

332 A mummied Fish, in a wooden case, made to represent a fish.

333. }
334. } Two Glass Bottles. From Sakkarah.

335. A Potter's model, in wood. From Thebes.

336. A small wooden figure of Osiris, seated. The body is hollowed and has a small mummy enclosed.

337. A wooden figure of Typhon, with a bronze bangle on each arm. From Ghiseh.

338. A figure of Osiris, similar to No. 331.

339. A Wooden Snake, the pedestal contains a mummy of the reptile. From the Fayoum.

340. Wooden representation of a Crocodile.

341. Represents Bubastes, the lion-headed god, in a sitting posture. From Lower Egypt.

342. A small wooden figure of Isis and Horus.

343. A wooden figure of the Ichneúmon, well executed. The pedestal contains a mummy. From Sakkarah.

344. Figure of a Fish, in wood.

345. Fragment of the figure of Typhon, in blue pottery.

346. Part of a Wooden Hammer. From Thebes.

347. A dove-tail of Wood, taken from the corner of the palace of Rameses the Great, at Medinet Abou, the most southerly ruin of Thebes, on the left bank of the Nile, about 1355 years B. C., used to connect the stone-work.

348. A similar but smaller piece of Wood. From the temple at Karnac.

349. An earthenware head of Typhon.

350. A piece of dark wood, inscribed with two lines of hieroglyphics.

351. A Drill-bow, and Cord. From Thebes.

352. A Drill-bow. From Sakkarah.

353. A small figure of a Fish, in wood. From Sakkarah

354. A wooden Bull, very ancient and in very bad condition

355. A wooden Pulley. From Thebes.

356. The Mummy of a young Crocodile, unwrapped taken from the Crocodile Pits, at Manfalont.

"The Crocodile was sacred, and having no tongue, is a fit emblem of the Deity, since the divine reason needs no utterance, but governs all in silence. Its eye, when in the water, is covered with a membrane through which it sees, but cannot be seen, as the Deity beholds all things, being invisible."—*Vide* KENRICK, p. 16, Vol. II.

357. Mummied Snakes.

358. Mummied Crocodiles, similar to 356, but not unwrapped. From Manfalont.

359. A sacred Ibis, divested of its wrappings.

360. Two sacred Ibises, in their original bandages.

360½. Six large Crocodiles, from the Crocodile Mummy Pits near Manfalont.

361. Fragment of a Walking-stick, on which there is engraved a line of hieroglyphics, preceded by a man in the act of adoring the Theban Triad; probably in allusion to the office of the possessor, whose name and titles are contained in the inscription. This stick is ornamented with an ivory top. From Thebes.

362. Fragment of another Stick, with an inscription.

The heads of the Tribes of Israel had their names inscribed on their staffs, (Numb. xvii. 2,) and it would appear that the heads of families in ancient Egypt also practised this custom, for the chief person in the representations on the walls of the ancient tombs, has always a staff. All these sticks are much longer than the modern stick. From Thebes.

363. A Walking-stick, inscribed with the owner's name.

364. A Tally-stick.

365. A Stick made of wood, resembling that used in England for whips. It is extremely tough and full of knots.

This kind of stick is usually about four feet long, and has always a little branch near the top. It was carried by a certain class of persons attending funerals. This specimen has a bronze ferule at the thicker end, which, contrary to modern fashion, was the part that was brought in contact with the ground. It has likewise an inscription a little below where the hand would be placed. From Thebes.

366. } Two Sticks used to carry packages, similar to the
367. } net suspended over the Bulls, between two men; each end of the stick resting on the shoulder of the carriers.

368. A Papyrus, in the Demotic character. From Sakkarah.

369. Fragment, in basaltic stone, of a Sarcophagus taken from Colonel Campbell's tomb, or rather from one of the excavations in the trench which surrounds it. From Ghiseh.

370. } Pedestals, supporting a set of Stone Sculptures from
371. } the Tomb of Assa, in Sakkarah.

The hieroglyphics are most exquisitely cut in high relief, and the second stone is interesting from the portrait, which is evidently not an Egyptian. Assa was one of the Hyksos

372. A sandstone Tablet, representing two men making offerings of fruit. The sculptures are in relief and well executed. From Sakkarah.

373. A Papyrus, in the Demotic character, of the time of Cleopatra and Ptolemy. It is a contract for the sale of land.

374. } Two Papyri, similar to the above. From Sakkarah.
375. }

376. A piece of Cloth, painted in very bright colours, taken from a Mummy. From Sakkarah.

377. A limestone Tablet, representing one man leading a cow; another slaughtering a cow, probably intended as offerings to the deity.

378. A limestone Monument, representing a figure, in relief, receiving offerings. From Ghiseh.

379. A sandstone Slab, most exquisitely carved, in relief. From its style must be very ancient. From Ghiseh.

380. A painted Stone. The inscription is in the Demotic character. From Thebes.

381. A Funereal Papyrus in hieroglyphics. From Sakkarah.

382. A specimen of ancient Cloth. From Sakkarah.

"Their habits, which they called Calasiris, are made of linen and fringed at the bottom. Over this they throw a shawl made of white wool. (See No. 9.) But, in these vests of wool, they are forbidden by their religion, either to be buried, or to enter any sacred edifice."—Vide HERODOTUS, Euterpe, LXXXVI.

383. A Papyrus in the Demotic character. From Sakkarah

384. Three pieces of a Greek Papyrus. From Dashour.

385. Fragments of a Papyrus, found around the hips of a male mummy. From Sakkarah.

386.} 387.} The Wheel and Tire, and other portions of a Chariot, found in a Mummy Pit, near Dashour.

The wheel has six spokes, like those chariots represented in the paintings and sculptures. This, however, appears to be somewhat differently constructed, for it seems to have been strengthened by an inner circle.

388. A War Club, studded with iron spikes. Very rare. From Sakkarah.

389. Vases of Egyptian alabaster and black marble, mostly from Sakkarah.

The one upon which the number is placed is the most interesting, as it is beautifully carved, and also has the hieroglyphical numerals for nineteen, under the left handle; denoting, that it contains nineteen measures of that period.

390. The bottom of a Mummy Case, painted in water colours, which, notwithstanding its great age and continual exposure, are still very bright. From Sakkarah.

391. The cover of a Mummy Case. The dress is uncommon. From Sakkarah.

392. A gilded figure of Bubastes, decorated with a necklace of beads. From Sakkarah.

393. Two small wooden Obelisks inscribed with hieroglyphics. They somewhat resemble Cleopatra's Needle, at Alexandria. From Ghiseh.

394. An Osirian figure. From Ghiseh.

395.} 396.} Two instruments of wood, used in preparing clay for making bricks. They are also used as hoes for agricultural purposes. They are still retained by the natives. From Thebes

397. A Bull's Head, beautifully carved in wood, and ornamented with ivory. From Ghiseh.

398. A Common Barge for carrying cargo, with a crew of thirteen men.

399. A Mummy Case, containing a male Mummy. From Ghiseh.

400. A very handsome Mummy, supposed to be of a female Her head-dress is composed of Lotus flowers. From Thebes.

401. A magnificent Mummy of a young priest. From Thebes.

401½. Two Jackals, the emblems of Anubis, the guardian of the tombs. From Sakkarah.

402. A Mummy in a very splendid case. From Sakkarah

403. A Boat with its Crew, one of them propelling the boat with a long pole, as is the custom on the Nile. From Thebes.

404. A wooden figure of Osiris. From Sakkarah.

405. A large wooden figure of Osiris. It is hollow, and originally contained a papyrus. From Ghiseh.

406. A wooden figure of Anubis. From Sakkarah.

407. Two Lizards in bronze, most exquisitely executed. From Thebes.

408. A box of Wood in the form of a temple, highly decorated, containing a coarse vase in which was the heart of a Priestess. The lid of this box is surmounted by a hawk with a gilt head. It was found with the Mummy of a Priestess, in one of the tombs of Sakkarah. This Mummy, which was lost in the Nile, was beautifully painted, and its face, hands, and feet were covered with gold leaf.

409. A Statue of Thoth, the most exquisite work of art in the collection.

This beautiful little statue is only two inches and a quarter high; is made of fine limestone, but has the appearance of polished ivory. It is in perfect preservation, and of the most ancient style of sculpture. From Memphis.

410. An Osirian figure in wood, highly painted. From Sakkarah

411. The upper part of a white stone figure in the process of manufacture.

412. An Osirian figure painted and inscribed with hieroglyphics. The face is gilt—the body is hollow, and contains the Mummy of a Snake. From Thebes.

413. The lower extremities of the figure No. 411. This is curious as it shows how these figures were prepared From Sakkarah.

414. An Osirian figure painted and inscribed with hierogly phics. From Sakkarah.

415. A Bow of curious structure, with the leather case that contained it and attached it to thé war chariot. It is covered with the bark of the cherry tree, like the wooden pipes so celebrated at the present time in the East. Four arrows made of reed and tipped with flint-stone, are suspended with it. From Sakkarah.

416. A small cylinder of flinty limestone used as part of a necklace, inscribed with the nomen and prenomen of Amenemha, of the twelfth Dynasty, 2080 B. C This is a very rare specimen.

417. A specimen of ancient wool. From Thebes.

418. A Lady's work-basket, which, when found, contained the following articles (to No. 430, inclusive).

419. Two skeins of Thread, and a small white glass Bottle.

420. A small brown Glass, figured.

421. The top of a wooden Box in shape of a Scarabæus, probably the box contained some unguent.

422. Two hollow porcelain Balls, coloured black and blue

423. A small wooden Toilet Box, with five compartments to contain the black powder called Kohl, used to blacken the eyelids, as in the days of Jezebel.

424. A Netting-needle charged with the original thread.

425. Two bronze needles; one blade of a pair of bronze scissors, beautifully fashioned in the form of a sphinx; a piece of linen in the process of being darned or mended; some bronze pins.

426. A Dress Comb in ivory, chased on the back.

427. A wooden Comb.

428. Four small Ivory Pegs, use uncertain.

429. A Spatula for spreading unguents.

430. Some false hair platted.

431. A blue hollow Cylinder used to contain Kohl for the eyes, has the prenomen of Amunoph III., and the nomen of his second wife, queen Taia. Amunoph began his reign 1430 years B. C., and is supposed to be the Memnon of the vocal Statue of Thebes.

432. A similar Cylinder to the above, but not inscribed.

433. Toilet-stand, in wood, in the form of a column, with a palm-tree capital, and has also the instrument for applying the Kohl. From Thebes.

434. A Toilet-stand, for containing the pigment called Kohl, for blacking the margin of the eyelids.

435. A Wooden Box with two divisions, used to contain Kohl. Fastened by the stick used for placing the Kohl on the eyelids.

436. A similar Box, with four divisions, made of blue porcelain and inscribed.

437. A Toilet-stand made in black stone, for holding Kohl and the instrument with which this powder is applied to the eyes. From Sakkarah.

438. The same of Porcelain, decorated with ornaments.

439. A circular Box made of the tooth of the hippopotamus, in the form of a cup, with a cover. From Sakkarah.

440. The same as No. 437, in marble.

441. An Alabaster Vase.

442. A Box in wood, in the form of the pod of some plant. It contains a bronze instrument.

443. A reed containing a metallic powder of a blue colour, probably used at the toilet. From Sakkarah.

444. A reed containing ointment for a similar purpose.

445. A wooden Box with a cover, in the centre of which there is a hole for inserting the instrument to extract the contents.

446. A cylindrical Box of wood painted white. The cover is contrived after the manner of porcelain teapots of the present time, with little projections to prevent its falling off.

447 The same as 443.

448. Similar to 440; in alabaster. From Sakkarah.

449. A Toilet Box in the form of a shell and has the cartouche of a queen.

450. A long bronze Pin, and three ornaments for the hair made of ivory. From Sakkarah.

451. A Box in form of a Gazelle in the attitude of rising. The body of the animal is hollowed, and the back is ingeniously made to open by turning on a pivot From Sakkarah.

452 A Toilet Box in the form of a Duck, the lid opening as in the above. The box is beautifully carved and inlaid. From Sakkarah.

453. A Box made in the shape of a Fish, in slate-stone. The eyes inlaid, opens as the others, on a pivot. From Sakkarah.

454. A Spoon in the form of a shell made of glass, coloured to imitate nature. From Sakkarah.

455. A Cylindrical Toilet-box, engraved and outlined, filled with some white composition.

It represents women in the approved position of the Egyptian dance, playing on various instruments. Bouquets of flowers are strewed upon the floor, and one of the women, as if to gratify all the senses at once, pours into the cup of the person seated, before whom the others are dancing and singing, some grateful beverage. A line of hieroglyphics encircles the upper part, and the usual ornament of the base of an apartment decorates the lower part of the box. This curious piece of antiquity was found at Sakkarah. But, both in composition and style, it resembles the best designs painted on the walls of the Tombs, at Thebes.

456. A Semi-cylindrical Toilet-box, beautifully carved, in hard wood, with a sliding cover. The interior is divided into compartments. From Sakkarah.

457. Fragment of a Spoon, in soft black stone. in the form of a Fish.

458. A Spoon, in hard wood, shaped like a cartouche. In the hollow is represented a lake with fish, and the handle is fantastically carved to imitate the Lotus. It terminates in the head of a duck. From Sakkarah.

459. The same, beautifully executed, representing a bouquet. The Lotus is more prominent than the other flowers. Found at Sakkarah.

460. The same, in hard wood, representing a Nubian woman swimming, sustaining in her extended arms a duck or goose, which is hollowed out and forms the bowl of the Spoon.

The head of this figure is most beautifully sculptured, and the hair fantastically dressed after the fashion of the Abyssinians. It was found in a tomb at Abouseer, with 260; 1430 B. C.

461. The same, in wood. The hair dressed in a different fashion, and the bowl of the spoon wanting.

462. The same as the above, in ivory. The head wanting. From Sakkarah.

463. The same, in the form of a Lotus.

464. A kind of a Spoon, in wood.

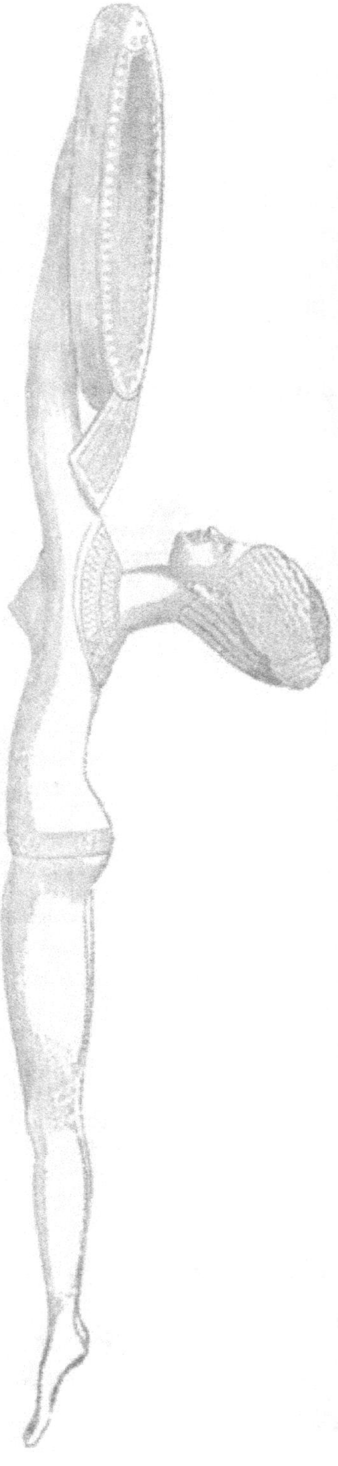

465. The same, in ivory, in the form of a fish. From Sakkarah.

466. Two cups of ivory, united.

467. A shallow Spoon, in wood, the handle of which is in the shape of a fox. From Sakkarah.

468. The same, with a varied device. From Sakkarah.

469. Instrument in wood, probably used for introducing some liquid through the nostrils into the head, in the process of embalming. From Sakkarah.

470. A small Toilet Box, in wood, in the form of a duck. Found at Sakkarah.

471. A beautiful and very rare Spoon; the bowl being formed of a shell, and the handle of iron, the only example of the kind I have met with. From Sakkarah.

472. Similar to 470.

473. Fragment of a Spoon made of marble, in the shape of a fish. From Sakkarah.

474. A Spoon made of ivory. The handle being a cow's head.

475. The handle of a Spoon in alabaster, in the form of the head and neck of a swan.

476. Utensil of wood in the form of a Lotus flower, its stalk and bulb. From Sakkarah.

477. A small Wooden Box, in which the gold ring No. 1085 was found. From Thebes.

478 to 481. Four Wooden Head-rests, or Pillows, inscribed, they all have the representation of Typhon on the pedestal, and on one the Hippopotamus-headed goddess, TE-OR, is engraved on the opposite limb.

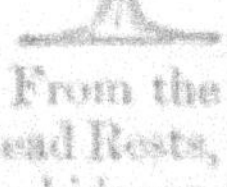

From the position in which these gods are usually represented on Head Rests, it would appear, that the ancient Egyptians considered the hideous forms of these divinities well calculated to secure repose, by frightening away the still more terrible creations of the mind. From Sakkarah.

482. Head Rest in stone.

483. Four small Vases. One of which contains some kind of unguent.

484 to 487. Bronze Mirrors, Nos. 484 and 486 have bronze handles representing the Goddess Athor. From Assouan

488. A small bronze Vase, surrounded with figures in relief. From Sakkarah.

489. A similar but smaller Vase.

490, 491. Two pairs of Bronze Castanets, used by the female dancers. By their side is a smaller one. From Sakkarah.

492, 493, 494. Three Wooden Combs. From Sakkarah.

495. A Bronze Key. From Thebes.

496. A Brush of Date fibre, for chasing away flies. From Sakkarah.

497. A Porcelain Drinking-Cup, in the shape of a Lotus. Coloured. From Sakkarah.

498. The head of Isis, beautifully carved in wood. From Ghiseh.

499. A Systrum in wood.

500, 501. Two similar Instruments.

502, 503. The same in blue Porcelain.

504, 505, 506. The same in Bronze. These instruments were carried in religious processions, and at the present time are used in the Christian Churches in Abyssinia.

507. A portable Balance. It appears to be cut out of one piece of wood, and has a piece of lead at its extremity as a weight. From Sakkarah.

508. A wooden Spindle. From Sakkarah.

509. A bronze Drinking-Vessel, beautifully made, has been turned and varnished. From Thebes.

510. A bronze Drinking-Vase, of a somewhat different form From Thebes.

511. A bronze Fork, used by the Priests in presenting offerings to the Pharaohs, when seated as Gods, on high thrones.

512. A similar Instrument. Both from Sakkarah.

513. A Packet not yet opened, found with the grain. Sakkarah.

514. A Wild Duck, cut down the back, salted and spread out for dried provisions. Found with some others in a jar, at Thebes, by A. C. Harris, Esq.

515. A bronze Colander, beautifully made. Found near Heliopolis.

516. A small Porcelain Vase.

517. Basket made of the small ends of the Papyrus leaf, containing fruit. From Thebes.

518, 519. Pieces of bread found in the Tombs, deposited with the dead. From Thebes.

520. A small Vase containing gum.

521. A small Vase containing lees.

522. An earthen Jar containing fruit and seeds. From Thebes.

523. A Package containing wheat. A sample of which is placed upon the table. From Sakkarah.

524. A small Stand or Table made of a sonorous stone, is quite perfect, and finished with great accuracy. Stands, of this form, set in rows, and laden with fruit and viands of various descriptions, are represented in the more ancient Tombs. This is one foot in diameter, and was found in a tomb, at Sakkarah.

525. A Net containing the fruit of the Persea, and of a species of palm, now nowhere to be found in the Valley of the Nile, but which grows abundantly in some of the Valleys of the Bisharean desert, between Korosko and Aboo-Hamed. A specimen of each of these fruits lies in front of the net. From Thebes.

526. An earthenware Vase containing fruit and seeds. From Thebes.

527. A similar Vase, which has been covered with rope netting; containing fruits, &c

528. Grain from No. 523.

529. Sample of Grain from the Tombs at Thebes, presented by Sir Gardner Wilkinson.

530. A handsome marble Vase, containing mummied eggs found in the large Vase No. 2, in the Egg Pits at Sakkarah.

531. Lotus leaves found under the head of a female Mummy. At Thebes.

532. A Fruit from the Tombs. At Thebes.

532½. A mummied Goose. From Sakkarah.

533. A set of Reed Pens and a bronze Knife found at Abouseer.

534, 535. Tablets used by the Egyptian children in learning to write the Greek language, when first introduced by the Ptolemies. From Abouseer.

536, 537. Two sets of Tablets, covered with black wax, used for the same purpose as the above; also, the bronze stylus employed in writing. From Abouseer.

538. A kind of Tee-to-tum in stone, with the Greek alphabet inscribed thereon, supposed to have been used by children, to learn their letters, as it was found with the above tablets.

539. A Stone Marble.

540. An earthenware Toy.

541. A set of Wooden Dolls.

542. Seven pieces of Wood, probably used by children in some game, resembling one now very common in Egypt. One side of each stick is deprived of its bark, and according to the manner in which they fall, the bark or the contrary side upwards, the game is won or lost. From Sakkarah.

543. Four small Vases, of terra-cotta, in shape similar to those from which libations were poured. It was found with a Mummy of the Ptolemies. From Sakkarah.

544. Square Tablet of wood, with an enchohorial inscription. From Sakkarah.

545. A Painter's Stone and Muller for grinding colours

546. Pallet or Inkstand of a Scribe, in wood.

This instrument not only served to contain the brushes or reeds used in writing, and the black and red pigments, but was also used as a tablet and ruler. From Thebes.

547, 548. The same as the above.

549. A similar Pallet, but smaller, and in green porcelain.

550. A Scribe with one of the above pallets in his right hand, and a roll of papyrus in his left hand, in porcelain.

551. A Shell and Brush, probably used by a painter.

552. A small stone Pallet.

553. The same as No. 543.

554. A small leaden Vase. From Sakkarah.

555. An instrument in wood, in the form of the hind leg of a gazelle, used for polishing. From Sakkarah.

556. The lid of a box in lead, it has a bronze hinge.

557. A curved packing-needle of wood. From Sakkarah.

558. An iron instrument, with a wooden handle. From Sakkarah.

559. Specimens of the Papyrus and other reeds.

560. Lid of the small Sarcophagus, No. 561, which contains the effigies of two Mummies, and was probably used as mentioned by Herodotus, Euterpe LXXVIII.

562. Model of a Boat in green porcelain, containing nine persons and some animals. From Thebes.

563. A Lion's head beautifully carved in wood. From Thebes.

564. A piece of the pasteboard cover of a Mummy, painted and varnished.

565. A piece of Wood with Greek and Enchorial inscriptions. From Thebes.

566. The figure of a Monkey, curiously pressed out of folds of linen. From Sakkarah.

567. Cotton Cloth found by S. Potts, Esq., at Petræa, in 1844.

570.

568. A vase in the form of Typhon. From Sakkarah.

569. A Figure used in the Game of Chess. From Sakkarah.

570. Curved stick, such as is seen in the hand of the hunter in the representations of this ancient diversion, in the older tombs. It was used for throwing at birds, and by its form probably partook of the Beaumerang of the New Hollanders, or the Trombash still in use in the interior of Africa.* This sample is inscribed and bears the cartouche compounded of the word AMUN, and other characters terminating in the ◠ feminine article. The cartouche is preceded by the title "Royal Daughter." Perhaps this instrument was used also by the ladies of these heroic times, who, in the representations above quoted, are frequently seen accompanying their fathers or husbands in a small boat made of papyrus, in which it appears the ancient Egyptians navigated the canals or smaller branches of the parent stream—which in those days, particularly in the Delta, abounded in the papyrus plant. There is a bronze nail at the top of the handle. This remarkable instrument was found in a tomb at Thebes.

571. A small Bow with the original Cord.

572. A Cow's Horn, much bent, closed at the bottom with a circular piece of wood, and open at the narrow end so as to form a kind of scoop or spoon. From Sakkarah.

* The Trombash is used also in war, and made of iron, and more curved than the Beaumerang of the New Hollanders.

570.

573. An oblong Box with a drawer, containing 21 pieces of Porcelain, half the number of different shapes. One side of the box is divided into thirty squares, the other into twenty, apparently for playing different games. From Thebes.

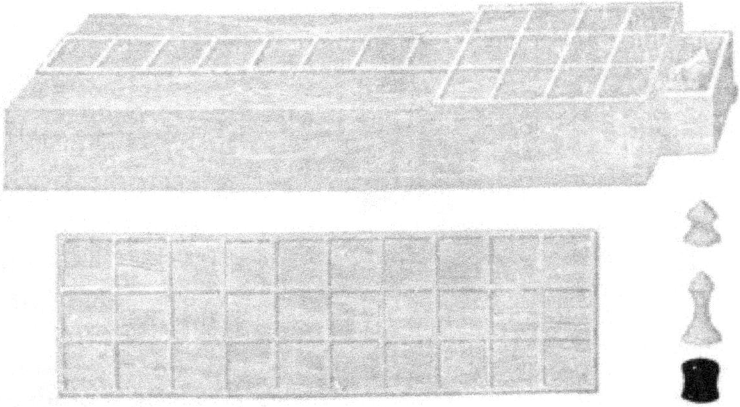

574 Iron Helmet, with a neck-guard in chain armour. This rare article was found at Thebes, with the following,

575 Fragment of a Breast-plate, made of pieces of iron in the form of scales, one of which takes the shape of a cartouche, and has stamped thereon the name of the Egyptian king Shishak, who invaded Jerusalem 971 years B. C. See 1 KINGS, ch. 14, v. 25; 2 CHRONICLES, ch. 12, v. 2.

576. An Iron Spatula. From Sakkarah.

577. An Arrow Head in iron, found with Nos. 574 and 575

578. Model of an Instrument, partly in wood and partly in steel, shaped like the hieroglyphic symbol used in the prenomen of Rameses. Also, a small Statue of Horus, and an instrument having a lion's head, the lower extremity of which is forked. These, and the helmet and breast-plate, are very rare and are the only articles *in iron or steel*, of undoubted antiquity, and are not to be found in any other collection. The rarity of this metal is, however, to be attributed rather to the rapid decomposition it undergoes when exposed to damp, than to ignorance

of its properties; for besides that it is recorded to have been known to the antediluvians, (see GENESIS, ch. 4, v. 22,) it is more universally abundant than any other metal; and it would have been impossible to execute such works as are found in both Egypt and Greece, without its aid.

579.

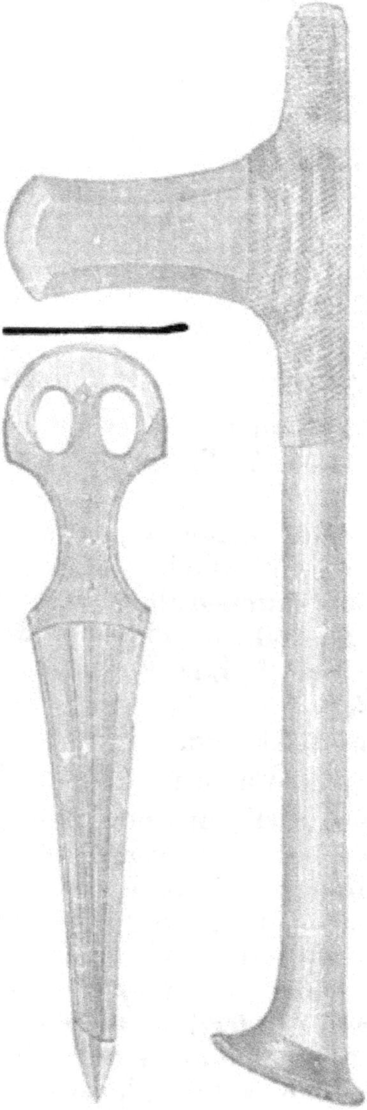

A Battle-axe, beautifully made of bronze, firmly bound to its original handle by means of slender interlaced thongs of leather From Thebes.

580.

A bronze Dagger, with Horn Handle attached to the blade by silver rivets. This dagger is beautifully made, and resembles much those carried by the Nubians of the present period From Thebes

581. A Stick used in hurling a stone from a sling

582,
583, Sticks said to be used for throwing at small birds.
584.

585. Handle of a Dagger, in Lapis Lazuli, bearing the cartouche of Osirei, 1385 years B. C. From Sakkarah.

586. Vase of red stone, of the quality of "Rosso Antico." From Sakkarah.

587. A small alabaster Vase.

588. A fragment of Pottery of the Ptolemaic period. From Sakkarah.

589. A small alabaster Vase. From Sakkarah.

590. A fragment of an earthenware Vase, representing an infant clasped in the arms of a female. From Sakkarah.

591. A Vase of a hard green stone, of oval shape, and with a small spout, resembling a gourd cut in half. From Sakkarah.

592. An Ivory Figure. From Abouseer.

593. An Ivory Figure. do.

594. An earthenware Stamp, with a royal name.

595. A large wooden Stamp, in the shape of a cartouche, inscribed. Mr. Oswald gives the following as a translation: "The Priest of Phath, the great god (Macrobius: the keeper of the house of gifts of Osiris, the Lord of the West.

596. A representation of a Lotus, in coloured pottery. From Sakkarah.

597. A Stamp, in the shape of a cartouche, in blue pottery. Inscribed. From Sakkarah.

598. A stamp in stone, inscribed with the name of Amunoph. From Thebes.

599. Prenomen of the father of Sesostris, in porcelain. The oval, which encircles the name, represents a double rope: the whole is a good example of the style of hieroglyphics of his tomb, and age, 1395 years B. C. From Sakkarah.

600. The figure of a God seated, in blue porcelain. From Sakkarah.

601. A small Tablet, in form of a temple, having the Bul Apis in relief, in porcelain. From Sakkarah.

602. A Bone carved. From Sakkarah.

603. A piece of Ivory, beautifully carved. From Sakkarah.

604. A Wedge in ivory.

605. A specimen of Porcelain. A fragment.

606. Fragments of a Cartouche, in glazed porcelain.

607. A Vase similar to the Etruscan. From Sakkarah.

608. An alabaster Cup.

609. An alabaster Jug.

610. A small Vase, apparently Etruscan. Sakkarah.

611. Two elegantly shaped Vases, in different coloured glass. From Sakkarah.

612. Representation of a heart-shaped Vase. It is of green stone, and is beautifully inscribed with hieroglyphics.

613. Representation in red agate, of the knot or tie of the girdle worn by the gods, kings, and priests. The back is beautifully inscribed in hieroglyphics, and was taken from the same mummy as the heart shaped Vase, No. 612.

614. A Vase similar to 612.

615. A piece of Agate inscribed, similar to No 613.

616. A white Stone, curiously carved with the head of Osiris, and has been suspended by a bronze loop, which is inserted into the head. From Sakkarah.

617. A Fish blown in white glass. From Sakkarah.

618. An oval-shaped piece of Green Glass.

619. Similar shaped piece of Glass. Hollow.

620. Green Glass. Solid.

621. } 622. } Small Rings of green glass, worn as bangles by children.

623. A large Ring of glass, worn as a bangle.

624. An Amulet, inscribed down the middle.

625. A representation of the Vulture, in relief, made of coloured glass. The rest of the figures in this division are of similar manufacture. From Sakkarah.

626. A Chinese Vase, with 17 others of different forms. All found in tombs. Some from Thebes; others from Sakkarah and Ghiseh.

These Vases are curious, inasmuch as they prove the early communication between Egypt and China. *Vide* Rosolini. Sir Gardner Wilkinson's Manners and Customs—Sir John Davis' Sketches of China, p. 72, and Revue Archæologique, by M. Prisse.

627. A Chinese Padlock, found in the tombs at Sakkarah.

628. } 629. } 630. } 631. } Four Figures in wax of the Genii of Amenti. These are probably the oldest wax figures in the world. From Thebes.

632. A wax Bird found with the above.

633. The two Fingers in stone, from a mummy, the meaning unknown. Found at Sakkarah.

634. Ditto, ditto.

635. Fragment of Hard Stone of a brown colour, representing a part of the hand. The thumb is perfect, and most beautifully sculptured. From Fayoum.

636. 637. 638. Three Glass Disks inscribed in cufic; supposed to be money, very rare.

639. 640. Two small blocks of Alabaster, having the name of Psammitichus. 660 years B. C. Found at Sakkarah.

641. 642. 643. Beads made of coloured glass, each colour forms a layer. From Sakkarah.

644. A piece of Black Glass, with different coloured glass inlaid on the top. From Sakkarah.

645. Part of a bead Necklace. From Sakkarah.

646. A long Bead in different coloured glass. Sakkarah.

647. A piece of Mosaic Glass.

648. A white transparent glass Bead.

649. 650. Two blue and white glass Ornaments.

651. A Glass Ornament.

652. A small Glass Model of the Crown of Upper and Lower Egypt.

653. Two pieces of Green Glass, imitations of precious stones.

654. 655. 656. Three small blue glass Figures.

657. A small white Bottle. From Sakkarah.

658. A similar Bottle, from Colonel Campbell's tomb at Ghiseh.

659. Three small Figures in glass. From Sakkarah.

660. A grotesque Face in glass.

661. A grotesque Face in coloured glass.

662. Small coloured glass Figure of a grotesque form. Sakkarah.

663. A piece of earthenware with Mosaic, in glass.

664. The portrait of an Ethiopian King, in glass, wearing the Crown of Upper and Lower Egypt, which is of porcelain. From Sakkarah.

665. A small Tazza, in a hard variegated stone, most beautifully polished.

666. A basso relievo Figure, in blue opaque glass, highly polished, wearing a necklace of very minute pieces of variously coloured glass. This is a figure of the Goddess of Truth, who is often represented without a head. This is a very rare specimen. From Sakkarah.

667. A piece of opaque blue glass.

668. The Goddess of Truth, in opaque red glass.

669. A small Tazza of glass, of a beautiful emerald green colour. When found, it contained some rouge for a lady's toilet. From Sakkarah.

670. A Figure of a Monkey, in blue glass, and of good style and has the name of Pharaoh Nophrah, of the Scriptures. Apries, 596 years B. C. He took Sidon.

671. A diminutive Lion, in blue glass, very finely executed, and on the base has the prenomen of Amunoph III., the supposed Memnon of the vocal statue of Thebes. 1430 years B. C.

672. A white transparent Glass Bead, solid and filled with pieces of variegated glass, similar to the Venetian manufacture of the present day. From Sakkarah.

673. Six porcelain Beads, inlaid with blue and other coloured glass.

674. } Two pieces of Transparent Glass, inlaid with pieces
675. } of various colours. From Sakkarah.

676. A Screw, made of opaque blue glass. From Sakkarah.

677. A Cartouche in earthenware.

678. Three fragments of Coloured Glass, on a card.

No. 1 represents a Star; No. 2 a Lotus. These pieces are particularly interesting, as examples of a curious manufacture. No. 3 more especially deserves attention, inasmuch as it explains the ingenious manner by which the ancients accomplished the work. Long sticks of glass, of the desired colour and form, were welded together, side by side. This mass being well united, was then sawn through, transversely, at regular intervals; thus producing a supply of perfectly similar patterns. The pieces thus obtained were afterwards polished and inserted, like Mosaic work to decorate various utensils. Thus, for example, were produced a series of stars of exactly similar dimensions and form as No. 1, which were inserted side by side, in a cavity, to represent the heavens; or the ornament No. 2, representing the lotus, was thus reproduced with an exactness which no other contrivance could guarantee. The piece No. 3 has evidently been sawn from such a stick of glass as above described, and broken off. They were found at Sakkarah.

679. A small Tablet in chrysolite, inscribed in hieroglyphics of an excellent style.

680. A small stone Tablet, inscribed.

681. 682. 683. 684. 685. 686. Variegated Glass Ornaments. From Sakkarah.

687. 688. Two glass Imitations of alabaster. From Sakkarah.

689. A porcelain Figure of the Goddess of Truth, with the feather of Truth on her head. From Sakkarah.

All the other unnumbered Figures are of the same material, and from Sakkarah.

690. A Metal Bead found in a mummy case at Sakkarah.

691. An Alabaster Vase. From Sakkarah.

692. An Alabaster Vase and Cover.

693

693. An Alabaster Vase with the Cartouche of Ounas, 1920 years B. C.

694. An Alabaster Vase.

695. An Alabaster Vase and Cover, inscribed with the Cartouche of Papi, 2d Dynasty, 2001 years B. C. Abraham arrived in Egypt 1920 years B. C. From Thebes.

696. A small Alabaster Vase of the same date as the above. From Sakkarah.

697. An Alabaster Vase.

698. Alabaster Vase marked with the name of NO-PHRE-KA-RA, of the 2d Dynasty, 2209 years B. C. From Sakkarah.

699. An Alabaster Vase. From Sakkarah.

700. A Fragment of Limestone, inscribed in the arrow headed character. From Nineveh.

701. A Fragment of the Ivory Throne, from Nineveh. Presented by the Rev. Mr. Badger, who was present when the throne was found by Mr Layard.

702. An Ivory Figure found at Nineveh.

703. Ivory Figures, ditto.

704. A small Stone Cylinder, inscribed with the arrow headed character. From Nineveh.

705. An Ivory Head. From Nineveh.

706. A blue Porcelain Figure of NOPHRAATHOM.

707. A small Fish in blue porcelain.

708. Two figures of Pthah Soccaris, the god of Memphis

709. A sitting figure of Bubastes.

710. A fragment in blue porcelain, of Isis.

711. A grotesque Head in blue porcelain.

712. A beautiful head of Isis, in porcelain.

713. A porcelain Figure of Horus.

714. A curious figure of Pthah, in porcelain.

715. A Figure of the god Moi.

716. A piece of Mosaic of the Cartouche of Psammitichus II. 600 years B. C. Captivity of Jehoiakim, 599 years B. C. See 2 KINGS, ch. 23, v. 35, also ch. 24. See 2 CHRONICLES, 36 ch.

717. A small figure of Isis.

718. A Fish, in blue porcelain.

719. A curious figure of Typhon standing upon two Crocodiles, and having a Scarabæus upon his head, a goddess on each side, and another with outspread wings at his back.

720. A Sphinx.

721. Figure of a Crocodile with a hawk's head.

722. A Comic Face, in clay.

723. A Scarabæus inscribed with seven rows of hieroglyphics.

724. A large Scarabæus in green marble, with eight rows of hieroglyphics.

725. The same in limestone, with six rows of hieroglyphics.

726. A large Scarabæus in blue porcelain.

727. A large Scarabæus in blue stone, inscribed with six lines of hieroglyphics. From Thebes.

728. A large Scarabæus with the cartouche of Thothmes III., the Pharaoh of the Exodus. From Thebes.

729. A large blue porcelain Scarabæus, with ten lines of hieroglyphics, which have been filled up with a white composition, and has the cartouches of Amunoph III. and his wife. 1430 B. C.

730 A Scarabæus with seven lines of hieroglyphics, in dark green marble.

731. A Scarabæus in porcelain, glazed and placed on its back. Within the case are several other Scarabæi.

The Scarabæus was made an emblem of the Sun, because no female being found of this species, the male enclosed the new germ in a round ball and then pushed it backwards, just as the Sun seems to push the sphere of heaven backwards, while he really advances from West to East. *Vide Kenrick*, Vol. 2. p. 16.

732. A Human Face, in similar limestone to that of the figure of Thoth, No. 409. From Sakkarah.

733. A Necklace of beads from a mummy. From Thebes

734. The emblem of Stability. On the same stand are 189 figures of the Divinities of Egypt. The majority are in porcelain, and exquisitely executed, especially Nos. 1, 2, 3, 4, 5, 6, 7, 8, 9, 10, 11, 12, 13, 14, 15, 16 and 17.

735. A porcelain Sphinx, very coarsely made.

736. A String of coloured Beads.

737.
738. } A variety of Glass Beads.

739. An outline of Osiris, neatly executed. He is represented sitting on his throne as the judge of Amenti. This beautiful drawing is on a piece of fine limestone. From Sakkarah.

740. A limestone Tablet, with an inscription in the enchorial character. From Sakkarah.

741. A similar Tablet.

742. Tablet in dark red sandstone, dedicated to Osiris. The figures are all coloured. Thebes.

743. A Caricature, painted on a fragment of limestone, representing a Lion seated upon a throne as a king, and a fox, as high-priest, making an offering of a plucked goose and a feather fan. From Thebes.

744. Mould, in limestone, of a Bird. From Sakkarah.

745. A limestone Tablet, with some coloured figures in procession, carrying date branches in their hands. There is a line of hieroglyphics to each person. From Thebes.

746. Basso-relievo of a Goose and Lotus flower, well executed in limestone, coloured. From Thebes.

747. A green marble Tablet, inscribed in Linear hieroglyphics. From Sakkarah.

748. A small votive Tablet, dedicated to Ammon, for the cure of deafness. From Thebes.

749. The top of an earthenware Vase inscribed. From Sakkarah.

750. An Inscription, in Coptic, on a tile.

751. Inscription, in Greek, on a piece of limestone, and several other inscriptions. From Thebes.

752. Figure of Isis, beautifully carved in wood, and inlaid with glass or some vitreous substance. From Abouseer.

753. A beautiful specimen of Mosaic, from the same tomb.

754. A Figure of Isis and Horus, beautifully inlaid. From Abouseer.

755. A small piece of Mosaic Work.

756. **Green porcelain Vase of a flattened and circular form with an inscription of hieroglyphics cut on its edges Dedicated to Thoth. Thebes.**

757. } **Two glass Bottles. From Sakkarah.**
758. }

759. **Green porcelain Vase, similar to 756, but of finer material. The inscription is painted. From Sakkarah.**

760. **The skull of a Female Mummy. The hair and head-dress as when found at Sakkarah.**

761. } **The feet of a Lady with white leather shoes. From**
762. } **Sakkarah.**

763. **A Necklace of porcelain. From Sakkarah.**

764. **A broken Necklace, made of large black beans and cowrie shells.**

765. **Hair, of a yellow colour; does not appear to be human. From Sakkarah.**

766. **A magnificent funereal Papyrus, 22 feet long, most beautifully written in very small hieroglyphics, and finely illuminated. It is perfect, both at the commencement and at the end. From Sakkarah.**

This Papyrus is not only most beautifully written, but is finely illuminated with various illustrations, so that besides the written history of the life of the deceased, you have sketches illustrating the most remarkable events. In the first scene is represented the Sacred Bull, beautifully gilded, and the deceased supported by two or more Gods; in the next is the Hall of the two Truths, with the God Osiris sitting in judgment, assisted by the forty-two judges, who may be seen immediately above him; before him is the soul of the deceased accompanied by Anubis, the Guardian of the Tombs, and the Ibis-headed God, Thoth, who has been writing down the history of the departed, and has collected all his good deeds into a small bottle, which is placed in a scale, while in the opposite scale may be seen the Goddess of Truth, sometimes only the Ostrich feather (the emblem of truth) is used, weighing down the good deeds; this result having been made known by the God Thoth to Osiris, he awards such punishment as seems meet to him and his forty-two assistants, and the soul of the sinner is sent into purgatory, for so many thousand years, during which time he has certain labours to perform, which may be seen in the smaller illustrations; in the last sketch, the deceased is represented before Osiris awaiting his final judgment. If he has performed all the tasks imposed upon him to the satisfaction of the judges, his soul is allowed to return again to his body, (if it still be perfect,) otherwise he is sentenced to a lengthened residence in purgatory after which the soul is permitted to return to its original body and it is for this reason that the Egyptians were so very particular about preserving and mummifying the bodies of the dead.

776. }
777. }
778. } Bronze Vases. From Tel-el-Yahoudi.
779. }

780 A curious bronze Altar, for burning incense. From Tel-el-Yahoudi.

781. }
782. } Bronze Vases of different forms. From Tel-el-Yahoudi.
783. }

784. A very finely executed Hawk, wearing the crown of Upper and Lower Egypt, upon a bronze pedestal, which is supposed to contain a mummy or a papyrus. This figure is very scarce.* From Sakkarah.

785. A bronze Figure. From Thebes.

786. Bronze figure of Amunra, God-creator. From Memphis.

787. Bronze figures of Harpochrates. From Memphis.

788. Part of a figure, which ornamented some Shrine, and consists of seven sacred serpents erect. From Thebes.

789

A finely executed bronze figure of HAR-OERI, son of Osiris and Athor, and is frequently called the elder Horus. At Ombos he is styled resident in the eyes of light, Lord of Ombos, the Great God, Lord of the Heavens, Lord of Eelak, Philæ, &c., and is evidently connected with the Sun From Memphis.

790. A bronze figure of Isis. From Memphis.

791. A bronze figure of Athor, with the cow's head. This is a somewhat rare specimen. Among her many titles she was called Mistress of Dancing, the Cow engendering the Sun, &c. From Memphis.

792. A bronze figure of Osiris, the son of Netpe and Sed, and engendered of heaven itself.

In his struggle with Seth or Typhon, he appears to have fallen under the power of his antagonist, to have been defended by his son Horus, lamented by his wife Isis, and sister Nepthys, embalmed under the direction of Anubis, and justified by Thoth against his enemies. After the destruction and disposal of the limbs by Seth, his form was made again by Noum, (*Amon-Ra*,) the creator, on a potter's wheel. The most prominent function of Osiris is that of judge of the dead, seated in the hall of the Two Truths, with Ouem, (the devourer,) and the forty-two demons of the dead; he awards the ultimate destiny of the soul, perdition and darkness, or manifestation to light. See the drawing in the centre of the Funereal papyri, Nos. 51 and 766.

793. A bronze of Nofra Athon. From Memphis.

794. A bronze figure of a Slave Girl, kneeling, and her hands bound behind her. From Sakkarah.

795. A bronze figure of Phtah, the principal deity and protector of the city of Memphis, where he is represented in the form of Phtah Socaris. No. 708 From Memphis.

796. A bronze figure, with gilt eyes, of Pasht-Merephtah.

797. A bronze figure of Horus, who is styled Lord of the Abaton, and Lord of Memlak, Philæ. From Thebes.

798. A bronze figure of Har-Sont-to. Another type of Horus. From Memphis.

799. The heads of three Divinities conjoined. They are neatly cast, and are represented with their head dresses and necklaces. From Sakkarah.

800. A beautifully-executed Figure, in bronze, of the goddess Maut. From Thebes.

801. A beautifully-executed Figure, in bronze, of a man on a marble pedestal. From Thebes.

802.
803.
804. Bronze figures of Pasht or Bubastes. These figures are always well executed, some are from Memphis, and others from Lower Egypt.
805.
806.

807. Bronze figure of Phtah. From Memphis.

808. Bronze figure of Amon-Ra.

This God had a temple dedicated to him in the Great Oasis. He is not to be considered as the Ram-headed God, but it is one of the many forms which he assumes; he is the Great Creator, and is represented in the mystic chamber of the temple at Philæ, in this form, (painted blue,) seated at the potter's wheel, moulding the divine members of Osiris.

809. Figure of Osiris under the form of Khons. From Memphis.

810.
811. Small bronze Figures, similar to No. 795. From Memphis.

812. Small bronze Figures, similar to No. 798. Ditto.

813. A small figure of Horus as Har Ammon. Ditto.

814. A bronze figure of a God. From Memphis.

815. A bronze Figure, similar to No. 693. Ditto.

816. A bronze Figure of Smouth or Esculapius, the eldest son of Phtah. From Memphis.

817. A small bronze Figure. From Sakkarah.

818. A bronze Figure of a Priest. Do.

819. A bronze Figure, representing a Libatory Priest, holding in his hands an altar for libations. From Memphis.

820. A beautiful little figure in bronze, in a sitting posture. From Memphis.

821. A bronze figure of Typhon standing on a lotus, supported by two lions. From Memphis.

822. A beautiful bronze figure of Thmei, the Goddess of Truth.

She is represented with an Ostrich feather in her head, because all the wing feathers of that bird were considered of equal length, and hence meant true or correct. Sometimes Thmei is represented without a head, or blind, hence her impartiality and truth. From Memphis.

823. A bronze Bull. From Sakkarah.

824. A figure of a Cat with her Kittens. Do.

825. Bronze figure of a Cat sitting on a lotus. This has been the top of a staff. From Sakkarah.

826. Sacred Bull in bronze. Ditto.

827. A beautiful figure of a Cat, in bronze,—she has a silver necklace and ear-ring. From Sakkarah.

828. Bronze Cat.

829. Bronze figure of the Shrew Mouse, which was worshipped in the Temple dedicated to Latona. at Bootos.

This figure is said to have been assumed by Latona to avoid the pursuit of Typhon, and the Egyptians worshipped this animal and considered it sacred, from its supposed blindness, and regarded it as the emblem of primeval night and darkness. The goddess Latona was described as denoting night and darkness. From Lower Egypt.

830. A circular piece of bronze, beautifully ornamented. From Heliopolis.

831. A bronze Cat. From Sakkarah.

832. A Bronze Bull.

833. A Bronze Hawk, originally the top of a staff. From Sakkarah.

834. A Bronze Shrew Mouse. From Lower Egypt.

835. A small Cat in bronze. From Sakkarah.

836. Two Cats on a bronze pedestal. Do.

837. A clamp of Bronze, it is a very intricate and fine specimen of casting, it was one of four pieces used to protect the lower angles of a shrine, which was of wood. From Thebes.

838. } The two Horns of the Sacred Bull, Apis, found at
842. } Tourah, projecting out of the ground.
Vide Herodotus, Euterpe XLI.

839. A wooden cylindrical box, containing a bronze box or lining.

840. A piece of Bronze. From Sakkarah.

841. A large bronze Shrine filled with gum, it is beautifully engraved on each side with the figures of gods, it is very much oxydized. From Sakkarah.

843. An Ornament in bronze.

845. Bronze Instruments, used by mechanics.

846. A bronze Frog.

847. A bronze Fish Hook, found by Dr. Abbott, in a Mummy. From Sakkarah.

848. A bronze Mouse.

849. A bronze Stamp, in the shape of a cartouche.

850. A square Seal, inscribed with "the abode of Ammon," the hieroglyphics are in relief like type. From Thebes.

851. A small bronze Figure, similar to 786.

852. A small bronze Figure, similar to 798, only in a sitting posture. From Sakkarah.

853. A small figure of Horus. From Sakkarah.

854. A Cartouche in bronze. From Sakkarah.

855. A Plate of bronze, with the prenomen and nomen of TERAK, 714 years B. C. See 2 KINGS, XIX. *Terak*, or *Tirhakah*.

856. A thin plate of Bronze, with some unknown figures upon it.

857. Bronze Clasp of a waistband, taken from a mummy by Dr. Abbott. The rest of the band was of cloth, covered with circular plates of glass.

858. A bronze Ring.

859. Pieces of a Belt in bronze, from a mummy. From Sakkarah.

X. A bronze Lion.

Z. A bronze Sphinx. Both these figures are very rarely found in bronze.

860. Six bronze Knives.

861. Several links of a Chain, attached to a heart-shaped weight, cast in bronze. From Sakkarah.

862. Rings of bronze, worn as bracelets by the women of the lower order. From Sakkarah.

863. Bronze Statue of Athor, of the Græco-Egyptian period, in the attitude of the Goddess of Dancing *Vide* 791.

864. A large bronze Figure of a man. From Memphis.

865. A large bronze Figure of the Goddess NEITH. From Memphis.

866. Bronze Altar for burning incense. From Tel-el-Yahoudi.

867. Bronze Statue of Isis and Horus. From Memphis.

868. A statue of Osiris as judge in the hall of the Two Truths, as seen in the Funereal Papyri.

869. Finely executed figure of a Hawk, in bronze. "The bright and piercing eye of this bird made it an appropriate emblem of the Sun."—*Vide* Kenrick.

870. Bronze Statue of Isis and Horus. From Memphis.

871. Bronze Statue. From Memphis.

872. Bronze Statue of Horus. From Memphis.

873. A bronze, terminating in the head of a Ram. From Memphis.

874. Statue of Horus, in bronze. From Memphis.

875 A Sacred Serpent, in bronze, originally beautifully inlaid with some vitreous substance. From Sakkarah.

876. The Sacred Ibis on a bronze pedestal. From Sakkarah

877. Bronze figure of some royal person kneeling.

878. Bronze Altar, for burning incense. From Tel-el-Yahoudi.

879. The same as No. 877.

880. Bronze Ibis on a pedestal. From Sakkarah.

881. } Small figure of an Ibis, in bronze, with the ostrich feather (emblem of truth) in its beak.

882. A very small figure, of Amoun-Ra-Harsaphes. From Thebes.

883. A small figure of Khem.

884 to 891. A small drill and other instruments in bronze.

886. Part of the head-dress of Osiris, an ostrich feather in bronze, inlaid.

892. A very small bronze Statue.

893. Two Sacred Serpents in bronze, inlaid with glass or other vitreous substance of different colours. From Sakkarah.

894 A bronze figure of a Cat or Dog, apparently of the Persian Era. From Sakkarah.

895. Bronze Battle-axe. From Sakkarah

896. Bronze Figure of a woman grinding. From Sakkarah.

897. An Axe in bronze, found at Tourah where the Israelites were at work; supposed to have been used by that people. Upon the same shelf are other and similar instruments in bronze.

898. A figure of Osiris.

899. An Altar in bronze, with the stairs to ascend to it From Abouseer.

900. Statue of Khons, Phtah or Typhon. From Abouseer

901. Bronze figure of Anouph or Anubis. From Sakkarah.

902. A Pantheic figure with a lion's head. From Sakkarah.

904. Fragment in bronze of a God.

905. Small Figure in bronze, on a pedestal.

906. A curious Pantheic figure in bronze, representing Typhon standing on the head and shoulders of another figure.

907. Fourteen Bronze Arrow Heads.

908. A Mouse on a pedestal, originally the top of a staff.

909. Bronze Head-Dress in form of a Vulture. When worn by a goddess or a queen, it indicates that she is a mother goddess or mother queen. From Thebes.

910. A broken figure of an Ibis.

911. A bronze Throne, supported upon lions, with a figure kneeling before it. From Sakkarah

912. Figure of Horus.

013. Statue of Osiris.

914. An Ægis representing the head of Nouf. Temples for his worship were established at the Cataract of Syene, Elephantina, &c.

915. Figure of Isis, with outstretched wings, between two lotus columns, each surmounted by a Hawk. Before each pillar has stood a Jackal, but the front of this figure is unfortunately broken. From Sakkarah.

916. A Pantheic Figure. From Sakkarah.

917. Statue of Osiris. From Sakkarah.

918. Statue of Pasht. From Sakkarah.

919. Bronze figure of Pasht, encircled by the wings of a figure standing at her back. From Sakkarah.

920. Bronze figure of Horus. From Sakkarah.

921. Bronze figure of an Ibis. From Sakkarah.

922. Eight various kinds of Instruments in bronze. From Sakkarah.

923. Shrew Mouse in bronze on a pedestal. From Sakkarah.

924. Bronze Hinge. From Sakkarah.

925. The same as 923 but broken off its pedestal. From Sakkarah.

926. Two bronze Necklaces or Collars, worn by children.

927. Two bronze Rings, worn by children.

928. Bronze Knife, gilt. From Sakkarah.

929. Bull's head in bronze.

930. Small bronze Shrine, in which is Osiris.

931. Figure of Horus, curiously made of bronze and gypsum, in a stooping position, as if from age. From Sakkarah.

932. A coarsely made bronze Figure. From Sakkarah

933. Figure in bronze of Isis, with outspread wings. From Sakkarah.

934. Bronze Weight. From Sakkarah.

935. Bronze top of a Staff, terminating in a lyre. From Sakkarah.

936. A Cat's head in bronze. From Sakkarah.

937. A bronze Ornament.

938. Lamp in bronze.

939. Shrew Mouse in bronze.

940. }
941. } Two Vases in bronze. From Tel-el-Yahoudi.

942. An Ornament, representing an ostrich feather and sacred serpent on a Ram's horn. As seen represented in the head-dresses of some of the gods.

943. An Ægis in bronze.

944. An Ornament, somewhat similar to 942, inlaid.

945. An Ægis in bronze.

946. Part of the head-dress of Khons, in bronze.

947. A bronze Handle of a Drawer.

948. A bronze Bolt.

949. A Bottle. From Tel-el-Yahoudi.

950. A hollow Tube in bronze.

951. A Bottle similar to 949.

952. A bronze Nail.

953. The head and foot of an Ibis, the natural size, and most beautifully made.

954. A beautiful little figure of Nofre-Athom in silver. From Memphis.

955. A Case containing fragments of knitted head-dresses in cotton, worsted, and silk.

That marked A is of the latter substance. These are the only specimens of silk I have met with. In the bottom of the case is an ancient piece of bead net-work, originally taken from a mummy which it covered. From Sakkarah and Abouseer.

956. A Surgical Contrivance for covering an issue. This machine is far more cleanly, and much better adapted for its intention than the present system of bandaging, and is made of silver. From Sakkarah.

957. A Scarabæus mounted in bronze as a ring. Has the name of Rameses engraved upon it. From Sakkarah.

958. A large bronze Ring engraved. From Sakkarah.

959. A large bronze Ring having the name of Rameses the Great engraved upon it. From Sakkarah.

960. A blue porcelain Ring inscribed. From Thebes.

961. A bronze Ring inscribed.

962. A porcelain Ring, in form of a Cartouche, bearing the name of Thothmes III. From Thebes.

963. A small bronze Ring, inscribed. From Sakkarah.

964. Cylindrical Ring of blue glass, inscribed in hieroglyphyics; is capped at each end in the setting, which is in silver. From Thebes.

965. A small bronze Ring inscribed. From Sakkarah.

966. Do do do do.

967. Cornelian Ring, or rather that upper half of the ring which bears the inscription; the under half was probably made of metal, and attached to the above, in which there are holes made for that purpose. From Thebes.

968. A silver Ring engraved, representing a boat carrying the Bull "Apis." From Thebes.

969. An engraved Stone, supposed to be from Babylon although found in Lower Egypt.

970. Cornelian Stone, cut in the form of a Cartouche, and bearing the name of Rameses the Great. 1335 years B. C.

971. A red Agate, most beautifully engraved on each side, and round the edges.

On one side is the figure of the lion-headed God Bubastes, with an inscription. On the reverse is an inscription most beautifully cut, but whether in the Coptic or Greek language has never been determined. From Sakkarah.

972.
973. } Three Silver Rings. Found in Lower Egypt.
974.

975.
976. } A pair of silver Ear-rings. Found with the above.

977. A silver Ring, beautifully made to represent a serpent holding a ball or an apple in its mouth. From Memphis.

978. A Necklace in yellow metal, with pendants of pearls From Sakkarah.

979. }
980. } A pair of bronze Ear-rings. From Sakkarah.

981. A bronze Ear-ring. From Sakkarah.

982. }
983. } A pair of bronze Ear-rings, with stone drops. From Sakkarah.

984. A square Ring in silver engraved, and representing Amunoph II., (1456 years B. C.,) beheading his enemies. From Sakkarah.

985. A silver Scorpion, originally inlaid, and forming part of the head-dress of the goddess Selk. From Sakkarah

986. A small Tortoise, originally forming the head-dress of Las-an-ho, one of the evil genii, and called in the Rituals or funereal papyri, "the Guardian of the Third Gate," and is said to be fed with the limbs of his disturbers. From Sakkarah.

987. Fragments of a small statue of Isis and Horus, in a heavy metallic substance, covered with thin gold, probably an ancient fraud, as from the weight of the material, it might have passed for solid gold. From Sakkarah.

988. A small Scarabæus mounted in gold. From Sakkarah.

989. A thin plate of gold, impressed with figures of Divinities, taken, with others, from a mummy found by Dr. Abbott at Sakkarah.

990. }
991. }
992. } Plates of Gold similar to the above.
993. }

994. A Bracelet made of twisted gold wire, the ends terminating in a lotus flower. From Sakkarah.

995. A small gold Figure kneeling.

996. Head of the lion-headed God, in gold

997 to 1000. Figures of different Divinities, stamped in gold. Taken from a mummy, around the neck of which they were strung as beads in a necklace. From Sakkarah.

1001. An Ornament in silver gilt. From Sakkarah.

1002. A large Ear-ring, terminating in a bull's head; it is beautifully made of gold wire, and minutely decorated about the neck. It was originally ornamented with precious stones, which have been taken from the horns and forehead. From Thebes.

1003. A small gold Ornament, beautifully worked and decorated with several small chains, each terminating in an ornament resembling a small bottle; it is supposed to have been the drop of an ear-ring. From Sakkarah.

1004. } Two very small Bottles in gold, resembling those
1005. } used to contain the good deeds of the dead. From Sakkarah.

1006. Four Links of gold, supposed to be used as currency. From Sakkarah.

1007. A gold Ear-ring with a pearl. From Sakkarah.

1008. A small piece of Gold, supposed to be used as an ear-ring. From Sakkarah.

1009. A large gold Ear-ring. From Sakkarah.

1010. }
1011. } Two small gold Beads. Ditto.

1012 to 1020. Figures of Divinities, stamped in gold, originally strung together and placed round the neck of a mummy. From Sakkarah.

1021. Two gold Beads in the form of wheat. From Sakkarah.

1022. Two Beads in glass, *gilded.* From Sakkarah.

1023. A small plate of Gold, which formed the centre or clasp of a band worn round the waist of a mummy From Sakkarah.

1024. A small Scarabæus in pearl. From Sakkarah.

1025. A small gold Amulet, (broken.) From Sakkarah.

1026. A small gold Ring, in form of a serpent. From Sakkarah.

1027. A small Hawk in gold. From Sakkarah.

1028. A Gorget in gold. From Sakkarah.

1029. A gold Clasp, enamelled. From Sakkarah.

1030. An Ægis in gold, of the head of Bubastes. From Sakkarah.

1031 to 1036. Thin plates of Gold, stamped with various devices. From Sakkarah.

1037. A diadem in gold, prettily ornamented with the lotus flower, surmounted by the disk; in the centre are placed several circular thin plates of gold, taken from the neck of a mummy, around which they were placed as a necklace. From Sakkarah.

1038. } Two small thimble-shaped Ornaments, made of
1039. } gold and probably used as pendants, or drops to ear-rings. From Sakkarah.

1040. } The Crook and Flagellum carried by Osiris, in
1041. } gold. From Sakkarah.

1042. A large and exquisitely finished Scarabæus, in a hard green stone, by some said to be jade stone; it has on its under surface a thin gold plate engraved with eight lines of hieroglyphics, a prayer for the dead; it was found on the breast of a mummy, at Sakkarah.

1043. } Two figures of Typhon in gold, one of very superior
1044. } workmanship, found at Sakkarah, the other, in purer gold, was found at Thebes

1045. A Sacred Serpent in gold. From Sakkarah.

1046. A triangular plate of Gold, with a royal oval containing a name not legible; it was found on the mummy of a female. From Sakkarah.

1047. Two small plates of Gold, taken from the ears of a mummy.

1048. An eye in gold. It is used as the hieroglyphic of Egypt, and also represents the eye of Osiris. From .Sakkarah.

1049. A large Ring in the form of a Serpent. From Sakkarah.

1050. Gold Signet Ring, bearing the name of Shoofoo, the Suphis of the Greeks. 2325 years B. C. In shape and dimensions it resembles Figure 1, and the size of the impression exactly corresponds to Figure 2. Figure 3 is a magnified representation of the inscription engraved on it.

1

3

2

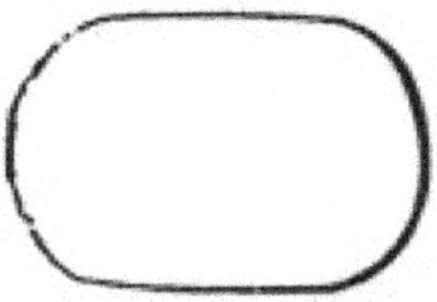

This remarkable piece of antiquity is in the highest state of preservation, and was found at Ghizeh, in a tomb near that excavation of Colonel Vyse called Campbell's tomb. It is of fine gold, and weighs nearly three sovereigns. The style of the hieroglyphics is in perfect accordance with those in the tombs about the Great Pyramid, and the hieroglyphics within the oval is the name of that Pharaoh of whom the pyramid was the tomb. The details are minutely accurate, and beautifully executed. The heaven is engraved with stars: the fox, or jackal, has significant lines within its contour: the hatchets have their handles bound with thongs, as is usual in the sculptures: the volumes have the string which binds them hanging below the roll, differing in this respect from any example in sculptured or painted hieroglyphics. The determinative for country is studded with dots, representing the sand of the mountains at the margin of the valley of Egypt. The instrument, as in the larger hieroglyphics, has the tongue and simi-lunar mark of the sculptured examples, as is the case also with the heart-shaped vase. The name is surmounted with the globe, and feathers, decorated in the usual manner; and the ring of the cartouche is engraved with marks representing a rope, never seen in the sculptures: and the

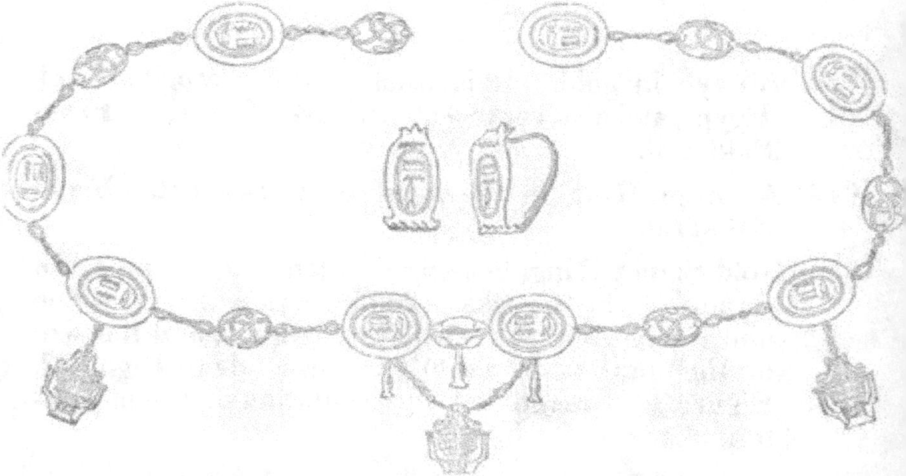

[illegible]. THE NECKLACE AND EAR-RINGS OF MENES THE FIRST PHARAOH OF EGYPT [illegible] YEARS B. C.

only instance of a royal name similarly encircled is a porcelain example in this collection, enclosing the name of the father of Sesostris. (See No. 599.) The O in the name is placed as in the examples sculptured in the tombs, not in the axis of the cartouche. The chickens have their unfledged wings; the Cerastes its horns, now only to be seen with the magnifying glass.

1051. A Ram's head in gold.

1052. Two Ear-rings and a Necklace, found in a jar at Dendera.

These ornaments are made of gold leaf, similar to that upon which hieroglyphics are usually stamped. There are three pendants of lapis-lazuli, and two beads of blue glass attached to the centre; where is also an oval amethyst bead, capped at each end with gold. But what is particularly curious is, that the name of Menes (the first Pharaoh of Egypt, who reigned 2750 years B. C.) is stamped upon the ear-rings, and upon eight oval plates of the necklace. These ovals have a dotted ornament around them. The circle around the ear-rings is plain, and is in the form of a cartouche. At equal distances between these ovals are curiously entwined devices, attached by a rude chain, formed of thin strips of flattened gold. There are also three pendants attached; they are in form of baskets, most beautifully executed, and will bear examination through a magnifying glass.

1053. An Ear-ring in gold, terminating in the head of a gazelle.

1054. A gold Ear-ring, terminating in a lion's head.

1055. A Scarabæus in gold, engraved with the name of the queen of Horus (Thothmes IV., of Sir Gardner Wilkinson). It was by this king's order that the great Sphinx was cut out of the rock, near the Pyramids, at Ghiseh, 1446 years B. C.

1056 and 1057. A pair of Ear-rings with a pearl drop.

1058. A small gold Ear-ring.

1059. A gold Ear-ring with a pearl drop.

1060. A small gold Ear-ring.

1061. A gold Ear-ring, with a drop in coarse emerald.

1062. A gold Ornament, in the form of a cow's horns.

1063. A very pretty gold Ear-ring.

1064. Figure of a sacred Bull, in gold.

1065. A gold Ear-ring, terminating in the head of a cow

1066. A sacred Bull in stamped gold.

1067. Part of a gold Ear-ring.

1068. A Gold Ring, in the shape of a Serpent.

1069. Part of a Gold Ear-ring

1070 and 1071. Two Figures of the common Fly, in gold plate; they have a piece of enamel let into their backs.

1072. A small Lizard of the desert, called the Warren, it is particularly well executed in gold.

1073. A spiral flexible Gold Ring, in the shape of a Serpent, set with carbuncles.

1074. A Gold Ring with two drop stones.

1075. The figure of Teor, the hippopotamus-headed goddess, in gold.

1076. The figure of Ra, the personification of the Sun.

1077. A massive Ring of fine gold, with a triangular pyramid of balls; similar rings are now sold at the Temple at Mecca, but made of silver, it being forbidden in the Koran, to Mohammedans, to wear gold ornaments. From Sakkarah.

1078. A Ring curiously made of six small porcelain Scarabæi, mounted in gold. It was found in the tomb of Assa, with the slabs, on the stand, No. 370.

1079. A Gold Ring surmounted with a pyramid cut out of some precious stone. From Sakkarah.

1080. A Gold Ring with a square shield.

1081 and 1082. Two Plates of Gold, inscribed with hieroglyphics.

1083. A Porcelain Scarabæus mounted in gold to form a ring; it has the cartouche of Thothmes III., the Pharaoh of the Exodus, 1495 years before Christ, according to Sir Gardner Wilkinson.

1084. A Gold Ring, engraved with some device.

1085. A Gold Ring, with the cartouche of Amunoph II., 1456 years before Christ. This ring was found at Thebes, in the small wooden box, No. 477.

1086. Ring of fine Gold, with the figure of the lion-headed God Bubastes engraved on two cartouches, each surmounted by the Ostrich feather, as is usual with royal names. From Sakkarah.

1087. A Gold Ring, in which are tastefully arranged two blue stones and one red one. From Thebes.

1088. A Gold Ring engraved with the Sacred Bull "Apis." From Sakkarah.

1089. A Gold Ring, engraved with the figure of Isis sitting; it is solid and of the shape called "Opisphendone." From Sakkarah.

1090. A large silver Ring beautifully engraved with the name of Amunoph III., 1430 years before Christ. From Sakkarah.

1091 and 1092. A pair of gold Ear-rings, hollow and minutely ornamented, one end terminating in a tiger's head holding in its mouth an engraved stone, and the smaller end in a hook which fastens into the gold setting of the stone. From Upper Egypt.

1093. Part of an Ear-ring in form of a cow's head, ornamented with a carbuncle set in the forehead. The head is curiously made of gold-leaf. From Sakkarah.

1094 and 1095. A pair of exquisitely-worked gold Ear-rings, terminating in a lion's head. From Upper Egypt.

1096. A small figure of a Bull's Head, probably a part of an ear-ring. From Sakkarah.

1097 and 1098. A pair of Ear-rings very similar to but smaller than 1094, '5. From Upper Egypt.

1099. A beautiful figure of a Bird with outspread wings, representing the soul departing from the body. This figure is in gold, beautifully inlaid with Turquoise and Lapis-lazuli, and it was taken from the breast of a mummy by Dr. Abbott, at Sakkarah.

1100 and 1101. A pair of Gold Ear-rings, beautifully made, terminating in the head of a gazelle. From Thebes

1102. An Ear-ring of similar construction, terminating in the head of a lynx, which receives the clasp. The expression of this head is very beautiful, the stone on the ring is a carbuncle. From Thebes.

1103 and 1104. A pair of gold Ear-rings, similar to 1100 and 1101.

1105. A beautiful little figure, in gold, of a bird, with a human head, and the wings expanded.

This figure represents the soul departing from the body, and is similar to one found in Etruria, and now in the museum of the Vatican. It was taken from the breast of a mummy by Dr. Abbott, at Sakkarah.

1106. A large coarsely made Ring in cornelian.

1107 A piece of Gilded Wood, inscribed with hieroglyphics. It was taken from a mummy opened by Dr. Abbott. From Thebes

1108. Figure, in gold, of a Bird with a human head, inlaid as No. 1099. The color of the mosaic is lost, probably from the heat applied in the process of making the mummy, from which it was taken at Sakkarah.

1109. Figure of Horus, in wood, gilt.

1110. A Cobra Capella, or sacred snake, in gold

1111. A figure of a God, in gold.

1112. A gold Ear-ring, with pearl drops.

1113. A Bird, with outstretched wings, wearing the crown of Osiris.

1114. A Human Head, carved in lime-stone, apparently a fragment of a built up figure; probably the head of a Sphinx.

This head was found at Benha il Assel, in lower Egypt. Benha is celebrated for its honey, and had the honor of supplying the prophet Mahomet with a present of honey when he entered Egypt. Hence its name, "il Assel," which signifies "*of the honey.*" Benha was the country residence of the late Abbas Pacha, who was murdered there in 1854

1115. The head of one of the Pharaohs, in white marble.

This was brought from Thebes by Dr. George Abbott. Being without date, it is not possible to assign it to any particular personage or era.

1116. The head of a King, from Benha.

1117. A small wooden Statue, from Thebes, having the name of Thothmes III. inscribed.

1118. A wooden figure of a Slave, with his hands bound behind him, and his face upturned, as though imploring his conquerors to grant him liberty.

1119. Cast in plaster of the Rosetta Stone.

The original of this cast in the British Museum, is a slab of Black Basalt, with inscriptions in three kinds of writing, known by the name of the Rosetta Stone, from the place where it was found by the French Engineers in the year 1799. It was by the help of these inscriptions that the hieroglyphical writing of Egypt, which had hitherto been an unknown character, was first read by Dr. Young and Champollion. The first inscription, which is in part broken, is in hieroglyphics; the second is enchorial, or common writing; and the third is in Greek. This last translates for us the others. It is a decree of the priests in honor of the young King Ptolemy Epiphanes, when he came to the age of fourteen, and was allowed to take upon himself the reins of government. It is dated in the ninth year of his reign, or B. C. 196.

1120. A very ancient Mummy, probably as early as the building of the pyramids of Ghizeh (say B. C. 2500).

Sent to America by Dr. Abbott shortly before his death.

1121. Menephthah III., or the Sethos of the XIXth dynasty, who succeeded in expelling the second invasion of the Shepherds of Phœnicia or Palæstine.

This plaster cast is from the full-length sand-stone figure in the British Museum.

1122. A small stone Sarcophagus containing the Mummy of a Cat.

1123. The Hand of a Female Mummy with a ring upon its finger. From Thebes.

Presented by Sidney A. Schieffelin.

1124. Piece of wood with a Greek inscription. From Sakkarah.

1125. Three small pieces of wood with Greek inscriptions. From an ancient Tomb discovered in Dongola.

1126. Fragment from the Great Sphinx.

1127. Petrified Wood from the Gebel Khashud, in the Suez Desert, southeast of Cairo.

Presented by Sidney A. Schieffelin.

CATALOGUE

OF THE

GALLERY OF ART.

No.	SUBJECTS OF PAINTINGS.	ARTISTS.
1.	**Portrait of** Luman Reed. (25 × 30.) Presented by the Artist. (*New York Gallery.*)	*A. B. Durand.*
2—6.	The Course of Empire.	*Thomas Cole.*

A series of five pictures, illustrating a nation's rise, progress, greatness, decline, and fall, and the consequent changes in the same landscape.

NOTE.—The isolated rock, crowning a precipitous hill, in the distance, identifies the scenes in each of the series; but the observer's position varies in the several pictures.

"First freedom, and then glory, when that fails,
Wealth, vice, corruption."

(*Reed Collection.*)

[FIRST OF THE SERIES.]

2. The "Savage State," or "Commencement of Empire." (61½ × 39.)

The sun is rising from the sea, over a wild scene of rocks, forests, and mountains, dissipating the clouds and darkness of night. Man, attired in skins, is seen engaged in the wild dance and the chase—the characteristic occupations of the savage life. In the picture, we have the first rudiments of society. Men have banded together for mutual aid. The useful arts have commenced in the construction of the canoe, the weapon, and the hut; and we may imagine the germs of two of the fine arts, music and poetry, in the singing usually accompanying the dance of the savage. The empire is asserted, to a limited extent, over sea, land, and the animal kingdom. It is the season of Spring—the morning of the nation's existence.

[SECOND OF THE SERIES.]

3. "The Arcadian," or "Pastoral State." ($62\frac{1}{2} \times 39$.)

Ages have passed; a change has been wrought in the scene—man has subjugated "the untracked and rude." We now see the shepherd and his flocks; the ploughman upturning the soil, and the wafting sail; by the shore a village, and on the hill the ascending smoke of sacrifice. In this picture we have agriculture, commerce, and religion. In the aged man describing the mathematical figure, the rude attempt of the boy in drawing; in the female figure with the distaff, the vessel on the stocks; in the primitive temple, and the dance of the peasants to the music of the pipe, we have evidence of the advance made in science, in the useful and the fine arts.

It is early Summer, and the sun has ascended midway to the meridian.

[THIRD OF THE SERIES.]

4. "The Consummation of Empire." ($75 \times 50\frac{1}{2}$.)

The rude village has become a magnificent city. From the bay—now a capacious harbor, with *phari* at the entrance, and thronged with war-galleys, and barks with silken sails—ascend piles of architecture, temples, domes, and colonnades. The massive bridge, the streets and squares, lined with palaces and adorned with statuary, clustered columns, and sparkling fountains, are crowded with gorgeous pageants and triumphal processions. It is a day of triumph—man has conquered man—nations have been subjugated. By wealth and power, knowledge, art, and taste, man has achieved the summit of human grandeur.

The sun is near the meridian

[FOURTH OF THE SERIES.]

5. "Destruction." ($62\frac{1}{2} \times 38\frac{1}{2}$.)

Ages have passed away since the scene of glory. Luxury has enervated, vice has debased, and the strength of the mighty nation has consumed away. A barbarous enemy sacks the city. The heavens are darkened by a tempest, and the storm of war rages beneath, amid falling walls and colonnades, and the flames of temples and palaces.

[FIFTH OF THE SERIES.]

6. "Desolation." ($61 \times 39\frac{1}{2}$.)

The moon ascends the twilight sky, near where the sun rose in the first picture. The last rays of the departed sun illumine a lonely column of the once proud city, on whose capital the heron has built her nest. The shades of evening steal over shattered and ivy-grown ruins. The steep promontory, with its insulated rock, still rears against the sky, unmoved, unchanged; but violence and time have crumbled the works of man, and art is again resolving into elemental nature. The gorgeous pageant has passed: the roar of battle has ceased; the multitude has sunk in the dust; the empire is extinct.

7. The Fortune-Teller. (52×42.) *William S. Mount*

Presented by the Artist.

(New York Gallery.)

8. Portrait of Myles Cooper, D. D. second President of Columbia College. Copy from COPLEY. (25×30.)

Presented by N. W. Stuyvesant.

9. Portrait of John C. Kunze, D. D. (25×30.)

10. Portrait of John Quincy Adams. (25×30.) *A. B. Durand.*

Taken from life, in 1834.

(Reed Collection.)

11. Portrait of John Adams. (25×30.) *A. B. Durand*

From the original by STUART.

(Reed Collection.)

12. Portrait of James Monroe. (25×30.) *A. B. Durand.*

From the original by STUART.

(Reed Collection.)

13. Portrait of John Wakefield Francis, M. D. (25×30.) *Charles L. Elliott.*

Presented by the American Art Union.

14. Portrait of William Cullen Bryant. (25×30.) *Henry Peters Gray.*

Presented by the American Art Union.

15. Portrait of Thomas Jefferson. (25×30.) *A. B. Durand.*

From the original by STUART.

(Reed Collection.)

16. Portrait of James Madison. (25×30.) *A. B. Durand*

From the original, by STUART, at Bowdoin College, Maine.

(Reed Collection.)

No.	SUBJECTS OF PAINTINGS.	ARTISTS

17. Portrait of Andrew Jackson. (25 × 30.)
A. B. Durand

Taken from life, in 1835.
(*Reed Collection.*)

18. Portrait of Egbert Benson. (22 × 26.)
John Wesley Jarvis.

From the original by STUART. See No. 611.

19. Portrait of Albert Gallatin. (25 × 30.)
William H. Powell.

Taken from life in 1843. Presented by the Artist.

20. Portrait of Daniel Stanton. (25 × 30.)
Charles L. Elliott.

Presented by the American Art Union.

21. Portrait of Prosper M. Wetmore. (25 × 30.)
Charles L. Elliott

Presented by the American Art Union.

22. Portrait of Seth Grosvenor. (25×30.)
John G. Taggart.

Painted for the Society.

23. The Chess-Players—Check Mate. (56 × 44.)
George W. Flagg.

(*Reed Collection.*)

24. Marine View. (36 × 25.) *Thomas Birch.*

(*Reed Collection.*)

25. Landscape. (36 × 26.) *C. P. Cranch.*

(*New York Gallery.*)

26. View from Froster Hill, England. (24 × 18.)
Andrew Richardson.

(*Reed Collection.*)

27. The Goblet and Lemon. (27×32.) *W. Van Aelst.*

(*Reed Collection.*)

28. Falstaff enacting Henry IV. (29×36.)
George W. Flagg.

Prince Henry.—Do thou stand for my father, and examine me upon the particulars of my life.
Falstaff.—Shall I? Content:—this chair shall be my state, this dagger my sceptre, and this cushion my crown.
King Henry IV., Part i., Act ii., Scene 4.

(Reed Collection.)

29. An Allegory — Death and Immortality — Antique. (18½×14½.) *Italian School.*

(Reed Collection.)

30. Portrait of Peter Remsen. (26×33.)
Samuel L. Waldo.

Bequest of Edward A. Newton.

31. Madonna and Infant. (16½×22½.) *German School.*

(Reed Collection.)

32. Bargaining for a Horse. (30×24.)
William S. Mount.

"Seth suspended for a moment the whittling his twig, and there seemed a crisis in the argument—a *silent pause* —when a shrill voice from the front gate adjourned the meeting instanter. It was the voice of Aunt Nabby herself, breathing authority and hospitality: —*Joshua, come to dinner, and bring the folks along with you.*" —*Jack Downing's Jour., N. Y. Gazette*, Oct. 28, 1835.

(New York Gallery.)

33. Portrait of Sir Charles L. Eastlake. (44×56.)
Daniel Huntington.

(New York Gallery.)

34. Landscape — Composition — Italian Scenery. (54×37.) *Thomas Cole.*

"O, Italy! how beautiful thou art!
Yet I could weep, for thou art lying, alas!
Low in the dust, and they who come, admire thee
As we admire the beautiful in death."
Rogers' Italy.

(Reed Collection.)

35. Portrait of Luther Bradish. (34×44.)
Thomas Hicks.

Presented by the Artist, 1857.

No	SUBJECTS OF PAINTINGS.	ARTISTS

36. **Flora.** (17½×22½.) *Jean Raoux.*

Presented by S. M. Chester.

(*New York Gallery.*)

37. Sleeping Female. (19×24.) *George W. Flagg*

(*Reed Collection.*)

38. Portrait of Clarkson Crolius. (24×30.)

Ezra Ames, 1825

Speaker of the House of Assembly, State of New York.
Presented by his son, Clarkson Crolius.

39. View of a Dutch Seaport. (48×26½.)

Presented by John McGregor, M. P.

40. The Vale and Temple of Segestae, Sicily. (65½×44.) *Thomas Cole*

"Midway between Palermo and Segestae, the broad slopes of an ample valley lie before the traveller. In the depth is a river meandering among fragrant oleanders; on the left the valley is intersected by a range of distant mountains; on the right is a beautiful bay of the Mediterranean. Across the valley, the mountains form a green amphitheatre, and high in a remote part is seen the Temple of Segestae."—*Notes of the Artist made on a Tour in Sicily.*

Presented by the Artist.

(*New York Gallery.*)

41. The Little Savoyard. (18×22.) *George W. Flagg*

(*Reed Collection.*)

42. Rebecca. (16×20.) *George W. Flagg*

(*Reed Collection.*)

43. Portrait of De Witt Clinton. (36×50.)

John Wesley Jarvis

Presented by the Heirs of Samuel S. Howland.

44. Portrait of the Earl of Carlisle. (44×56.)

Daniel Huntington

Presented by the Artist.

45. Portrait of Gen. Anthony Wayne. (24×29.)

Presented by George Folsom.

46. Portrait of James Rivington. (28×36.)

Presented by Samuel C. Ellis, M. D.

No.	SUBJECTS OF PAINTINGS.	ARTISTS
47.	The Truant Gamblers. (30×24.) (Reed Collection.)	*William S. Mount.*
48.	A Venetian Senator. (25×30.) (New York Gallery.)	*Cornelius Ver Bryck.*
49.	Portrait of Macready in character as William Tell. (25×30.) From the original by H. Inman. Presented by the Artist.	*Thomas S. Cummings*
50.	Interior—Dutch Apothecary Shop. (24½×18.) (Reed Collection.)	*Roelof Pietersz.*
51.	Pan and Midas. (24×28.) (Reed Collection.)	*Hubert Golzius.*
52.	Dead Game. (32×74.) Presented by John D. Clute.	*Adèle Evrard.*
53.	Portrait of Henry Abbott, M. D. (51×40.) Founder of the Egyptian Museum. Painted for the Society, 1863.	*Thomas Hicks.*
54.	The Black Plume. (29×36.) Presented by the Artist. (New York Gallery.)	*Charles C. Ingham.*
55.	Portrait of John Randolph of Roanoke. (22×27.) Presented by Washington Irving.	*John Wesley Jarvis.*
56.	The Pedlar displaying his Wares. (34×24.) (Reed Collection.)	*A. B. Durand.*
57.	Christ stilling the Tempest. (27×34.)	*Philip.*
58.	The Woodchopper's Boy. (25×30.) (Reed Collection.)	*George W. Flagg.*
59.	Wrath of Peter Stuyvesant on learning the capture, by treachery, of Fort Casimir. (30×24.) "On receiving these direful tidings, the valiant Peter started from his seat—dashed the pipe he was smoking	*A. B. Durand*

against the back of the chimney—thrust a prodigious quid of tobacco into his left cheek—pulled up his galligaskins, and strode up and down the room, humming, as was customary with him when in a passion, a hideous northwest ditty." *Knickerbocker's New York*, Book vi. chap. 2.

(*Reed Collection.*)

60. Madonna, Infant, and St. Ann. (29×28.)
Italian School.

(*Reed Collection.*)

61. Portrait of Rev. Samuel Provoost, D.D. (28×36.)

Presented, 1824, by Mr. and Mrs. C. D. Colden.

62. Landscape, with Figures. (24×20.)

63. Portrait of Rufus Wilmot Griswold. (20×24.)
Charles L. Elliot.

64. Portrait of Peter Van Schaack. (23½×28.)

Presented by Frederic de Peyster.

65. Portrait of John Jay, (1786.) (25×30.)
Joseph Wright.

Presented by John Pintard, (1817.)

66. The Match-Girl, (London.) (25×30.)
George W. Flagg.

(*Reed Collection.*)

67. Portrait of Peter Stuyvesant. (25×30.)

Presented by Nich. William Stuyvesant.

68. Portrait of Lafayette, (1825.) (25×30.)
Charles C. Ingham.

Painted from life in 1825, and is the *original* head from which was made the full-length portrait for the State, now in the State Department, Albany.

Presented by the Artist.

(*New York Gallery.*)

70. Portrait of John Pintard, (1816 — 17.) (25×30.)
John Trumbull.

Painted at the request of the Society.

No.	SUBJECTS OF PAINTINGS.	ARTISTS

71. Portrait of Daniel Seymour. (22×27.)
Thomas S. Cummings.

Presented by Robert Kelly.

72. Portrait of Rammohun Roy. (25×30.)
Rembrandt Peale.

Presented by J. K. Herrick, April 5, 1858.

73. Moonlight. (32×24½.) *Thomas Cole.*

(Reed Collection.)

74. Portrait of George Washington. (25×30.)
A. B. Durand.

From the standard original, by STUART, in the gallery of the Boston Athenæum.

(Reed Collection.)

75. Portrait of Gouverneur Morris. (28×36.)
Ezra Ames.

Presented by Stephen Van Rensselaer of Albany, (1817.)

76. Landscape, Moonlight. (37×25.) *Tempesta.*

From the collection of Cardinal Fesch.
Presented by Miss Eliza Hicks.
(New York Gallery.)

77. Lady and Parrot. (29×36.) *George W. Flagg.*

(Reed Collection.)

78. Portrait of John Quincy Adams. (25×30.)
Edward D. Marchant.

Presented by the Artist.

79. Portrait of Charles Fenno Hoffman. (25×30.)
Cephas G. Thompson.

Presented by the Artist.

80. The Nun. (24×30.) *George W. Flagg.*

(Reed Collection.)

81 Portrait of Robert Morris. (24×29.)
John Wesley Jarvis.

From the original, by STUART.
Presented by Thomas Morris, (1817.)

83. Mountain Stream in Western Va. (12×14.)
William McLeod.

84. Portrait of Christopher Colles. (10×12.)
John Wesley Jarvis

85. The Young Gourmand. (11×13.)
Frederick W. Philip
(*New York Gallery.*)

86. Portrait of James Kent. (25×30.)
Samuel F. B. Morse
Presented by John Delafield.

87. Portrait of Thomas Jefferson. (18½×26½.)
Gilbert C. Stuart.
Presented by David Hosack, (1828.)

88. Wreath of Flowers, encircling Coat-of-Arms and Miniature of the Duke of Austria, 1658. (33×46.) *F. Marrel.*
(*Reed Collection.*)

89. Lady Jane Grey preparing for execution. (45×56.) *George W. Flagg.*
"After uttering these words, she caused herself to be disrobed by her women; and with a *steady, serene countenance* submitted herself to the executioner."—*Hume*, chap. xxxvi.
(*Reed Collection.*)

90. Portrait of Catarina Schuyler. (32×38.)
Presented by Henry C. Van Schaack, Manlius, N. Y.

91. Portrait of Elisha Kent Kane. (51×42.)
Thomas Hicks.
Presented by Ladies of New York, 1859.

92. Portrait of Gevartius. (28×36.) From Van Dyck. *John Trumbull.*
(*New York Gallery.*)

93. The Mammoth Cave. (37×48.) *Regis Gignoux.*

94. The Sibyl. (25×30.) *Daniel Huntington.*
Presented by the American Art Union.

95. Portrait of Rembrandt. (25×33.) From the original. *John G. Chapman.*
Presented by the Artist.
(*New York Gallery.*)

96. Assumption of the Virgin. (25×19.)
Annibale Caracci.

(*Reed Collection.*)

97. Portrait of Aaron Burr. (8×10.) *John Vanderlyn.*

98. Portrait of Pietro Aretino, the Satirist. (31×37.) *John G. Chapman.*

From the original, by TITIAN, in the Pitti Palace, Florence.

Presented by the Artist.

(*New York Gallery.*)

99. The Image-Pedlar. (42×33.)
Francis W. Edmonds.

Presented by the Artist.

(*New York Gallery.*)

100. Portrait of Gov. George Clinton. (41×53.)
Ezra Ames.

Presented by George Clinton Tallmadge.

101. Game, Fish, Fruit, Vegetables, etc. (77×59.)
Francis Sneyders.

The two figures were probably put in by either RUBENS or JORDAENS.

Presented by T. W. C. Moore.

102. Portrait of Thomas Campbell. (25×30.)
Samuel S. Osgood.

Bequest of Rufus W. Griswold.

103. Portrait of Sebastian Cabot. (29×36.)
Cephas G. Thompson.

Painted at the request of the Society, from the supposed original by HANS HOLBEIN, which was the property of the late Richard Biddle, author of a Memoir of Cabot. A full account of the original portrait may be found in that work, pp. 317–320. It is supposed to have adorned the royal gallery at Whitehall.

104. The Dutch Bible. (22½×18.) *Cornelius ver Bryck.*

Presented by Daniel Huntington.

(*New York Gallery.*)

105. Portrait of Martha Washington. (22×26.)
A. B. Durand.

From the original, by STUART, in the Boston Atheneum.

(*Reed Collection.*)

106. Portrait of a Revolutionary Officer (Gen. E. Huntington ?) (20×24.) *John Trumbull.*

(*New York Gallery.*)

107. Tobias and the Angel Gabrael. (75×53.) *Rembrandt School.*

Thought to be by FERDINAND BOLL, one of REMBRANDT'S pupils, and a very successful imitator of the style of his master. He was born at Dort, 1611; died 1681.

This painting has been highly commended by connoisseurs and artists—among the latter may be mentioned the late lamented Thomas Cole.

Presented by T. W. C. Moore.

108. Portrait of a Young Lady, taken in 1608. (27×33.) *Flemish School.*

(*Reed Collection.*)

109. Portrait of Dr. Smalley. (25×30.) *John Trumbull.*

(*New York Gallery.*)

110. Landscape—Composition. "The Old Oak." (48×36.) *A. B. Durand.*

Presented by the Artist.

(*New York Gallery.*)

111. Portrait of Lord Lyndhurst. (48×50.) *Samuel S. Osgood.*

Presented by the Artist.

112. The Huntsman's Tent—Game and Dogs after a Hunt. (50×64.) *John Fytt.*

(*Reed Collection.*)

113. Portrait of Nicholas Fish. (25×30.) *James H. Shegogue.*

From the original by INMAN.

Presented by Mrs. Nicholas Fish.

(*New York Gallery.*)

114. Mother Child, and Butterfly.* (24×30.) *George W. Flagg.*

(*Reed Collection.*)

No.	SUBJECTS OF PAINTINGS.	ARTISTS

115. Autumn Scene—Conway Peak, White Mountains, N. H. (19½×14.) *Thomas Cole*

(Reed Collection.)

116. Dogs Fighting. (20½×16.) *George Morland*

(Reed Collection.)

117. Portrait of Thomas De Witt, D. D. (29×36.) *Samuel B. Waugh*

Presented by Theo. Cuyler, of Philadelphia, and Morris K. Jessup, of New York, 1858.

118. View on Catskill Creek. (24×16.) *Thomas Cole*

(Reed Collection.)

119. Landscape. (13×10.) *Dutch School*

(Reed Collection.)

120. Portrait of a Lady, (fancy.) (39×59.) *George W. Flagg*

Presented by the Artist.

(New York Gallery.)

121. Summer Sunset. (19½×14.) *Thomas Cole*

(Reed Collection.)

122. Old English Sportsman. (24×19.) *George Morland*

(Reed Collection.)

123. Murder of the Princes. (44×56.) *George W. Flagg*

ENTER TYRRELL.

"*Tyr.*—The tyrannous and bloody act is done:
The most arch deed of piteous massacre
That ever yet this land was guilty of.
Dighton and Forrest whom I did suborn
To do this piece of ruthless butchery,
Albeit they were flesh'd villains, bloody dogs,
Melting with tenderness and mild compassion,
Wept like two children in their death's sad story.
O thus, quoth Dighton, *lay the gentle babes,*
Which once, quoth Forrest, *girdling one another*
Within their alabaster innocent arms;
Their lips were four red roses on a stalk,
Which in their summer beauty, kiss'd each other.
A book of prayers on their pillow lay:
Which once, quoth Forrest, *almost changed my mind:*
But O, the Devil,—there the villain stopp'd."

(Reed Collection.)

No	SUBJECTS OF PAINTINGS.	ARTISTS
124.	Portrait of Philip Schuyler. (33×41.) Presented by Henry Van Schaack, Manlius, N. Y.	
125.	Miniature. (3×2½.) Dutch Enamel. *(Reed Collection.)*	
126	Boors Gambling. (10×7.) *(Reed Collection.)*	*After Teniers.*
127.	Wreath of Flowers, encircling Holy Family —Antique. (11×12.) *(Reed Collection.)*	*Italian School.*
128.	The Old Fiddler. (10×8.) *(Reed Collection.)*	*After Teniers.*
129.	Miniature. (3½×2½.) Dutch Enamel. *(Reed Collection.)*	
130.	Portrait of Hernando Cortes. (19×25.) Presented by Mrs. Gouverneur Morris.	
131.	Portrait of Americus Vespucius. (19×25.) Presented by Mrs. Gouverneur Morris.	
132.	Portrait—after Parmigiano. (30×40.) Presented by R. K. Haight.	
133.	Portrait—after Parmigiano. (30×40.) Presented by R. K. Haight.	
134.	Portrait of Christopher Columbus. (19×25.) Presented by Mrs. Gouverneur Morris.	
135.	Portrait of Fernando Magalhaens. (19×25.) Presented by Mrs. Gouverneur Morris.	
136.	Portrait of Frances S. Osgood. (25×30.) Oval. Bequest of Rufus W. Griswold.	*Samuel S. Osgood.*
137.	Landscape. (20×15.)	
138.	A Magdalen. (18×14.) *(Reed Collection.)*	*After Correggio*
139.	View near Bridgeport, Connecticut. (19×13.) *(Reed Collection.)*	*Andrew Richardson.*

140. Portrait of Alice Carey. (25×30.) Oval.
Samuel S. Osgood.

Bequest of Rufus W. Griswold.

141. Portrait of Henry Rutgers. (24×29.)

"Painted by the late HENRY INMAN, about the year 1828. The original I have in my possession, from which two copies were made by Mr. Inman and given to my uncle, Col. Rutgers; the one you have received, to his particular political friend, John Targee, and the other to the Rutgers College, at New Brunswick, N. J."—*Extract from letter of W. B. Crosby.*

Presented by P. R. Bonnett.

142. A Window-Scene. (14×17½.)

(New York Gallery.)

143. Portrait of Alexander Hamilton. (19×22.)
Charles Wilson Peale.

Presented by Duncan C. Pell.

144. Portrait of Lafayette. 1784. (19½×24.) Oval.

Presented by General Ebenezer Stevens.

145. Portrait of Capt. John A. Sutter. (14½×18.)
Samuel S. Osgood.

Bequest of Rufus W. Griswold.

146. Portrait of Lewis Morris, of New Jersey. (24×30.)

Presented by William A. Whitehead, Newark, N. J.

147. Portrait of Edgar A. Poe. (22×26.) Oval.
Samuel S. Osgood.

Bequest of Rufus W. Griswold.

148. Portrait of Cornelis Steenwyck. (9½×12½.)

Presented by Mrs. Eliza M. Clarke, of the Locusts, near Shrewsbury, N. J., 1856, through G. de Haert Gillespie, Esq.

149. Portrait of Fitz Greene Halleck. (20×24.) Oval.
John G. Taggart.

From the original, by C. L. ELLIOTT.

Bequest of Rufus W. Griswold.

150. Portrait of Rip Van Dam. (26×29.) Oval.

Presented by Mrs. Emily V. Goodwin.

151. Portrait of Mrs. Rip Van Dam. (26×29.)
Presented by Mrs. Emily V. Goodwin.

152. Portrait of John Stanford, D. D. (27×33½.)
John Wesley Jarvis.
Presented by Aaron B. Hays.

153. Portrait of John Watts. (27×34.) *John W. Bowles.*
From the original by HENRY INMAN.
Presented by J. Watts de Peyster.

154. Portrait of Richard Bayley. (18×21½.)
J. H. Lazarus.
From the original by STUART.
Presented by the Rt. Rev. J. Roosevelt Bayley.

155. Hector parting with his Wife and Child at the Scæan Gate. (42×48.) *Benjamin West.*
Presented by William H. Webb.

156. Chryseïs returned to her father Chryses. (42×48.) *Benjamin West*
Presented by William H. Webb.

157. Wreck of the Medusa. (77×50½.)
Jean L. T. A. Gericault.
Bequest of Uriah P. Levy.

158. Peasants Dancing. (77×57.) *Carl Bruner.*
Bequest of Uriah P. Levy.

159. Vision of the Archbishop of Rouen. (44×57.)
C. A. Vanloo.
Bequest of Uriah P. Levy.

160. Portrait of Mrs. Mary E. Hewitt. (25×30.)
Samuel S. Osgood.
Bequest of Rufus W. Griswold.

161. Portrait of Gen. William Irvine. (25×30.)
J. R. Lambdin.
From the original by ROBT. E. PINE.
Presented by W. A. Irvine.

162. Portrait of Charles P. Daly, 1848. (25×30.)
William Page.
Presented, 1881, by Mrs. Charles P. Daly.

NO. SUBJECTS OF PAINTINGS. ARTISTS

163. Portrait of Elihu H. Smith. (7×9.) Crayon.
James Sharples.

Presented by David Hosack, Feb. 19, 1833.

164. Portrait of Alexander Hamilton. (9×11.) Crayon. *James Sharples.*

165. Portrait of Samuel L. Mitchell, M.D. (7×9.) Crayon. *James Sharples.*

Presented by Dr. Samuel Akerly, Nov. 12, 1816.

166. Lago Maggiore and the Borromean Islands.

167. Portrait of Roger Gerard Van Polanen, 1831. (25×30.) *James Frothingham.*

Presented by S. Alofsen.

168. Portrait of Fitz-Greene Halleck. (13½×15½.) *G. W. Twibill, Jr.*

From the original by Henry Inman. See No. 606.
Presented by Mrs. Charles A. Davis.

169. Portrait of Daniel D. Tompkins. (58×90.)
John Wesley Jarvis.

Presented by Thomas E. Davis.

170. Portrait of John W. Francis, M.D., 1849. (25×30.) Oval. *James Bogle.*

Presented by the Artist.

171. Portrait of Bryan Rossiter. (25×30).
John Trumbull.

The first sergeant-at-arms of the N. Y. State Society of the Cincinnati, painted in the uniform of the Revolutionary Army.

Deposited by the N. Y. State Society of the Cincinnati.

172. Portrait of Mrs. Estelle A. Lewis. (25×30.)
C. L. Elliott

Presented by Mrs. Lewis.

173. Interior of the Park Theatre, New York City, November, 1822. (22½×31).
John Searle.

This water-color drawing of the new Park Theatre was made for William Bayard by an amateur artist; it represents the stage as occupied by Charles Mathews in the character of Morbleu, and Miss Ellen A. Johnson as Madame Bellegarde in Moncrieffe's popular farce of "Monsieur Tonson." The body of the house was filled by the artist with portraits of many of the most prominent citizens of New York at that time.

Presented by the heirs of Mrs. Harriet Bayard Van Rennselaer.

174. The Cavalry Charge of Lt. Harry B. Hidden. (75×45.) *V. Nehlig*

This gallant charge was made near Sangster's Station, Va., March 9, 1862. Lieut. Hidden, with fourteen of the 1st N. Y. Cavalry, charged a rebel outpost of one hundred and fifty infantry, driving them back, killing three, wounding five, and capturing fourteen. Lieut. Hidden was killed in the early part of the action.

Presented by William H. Webb.

175. Landscape. (8½×7¾.) *Thomas Gainsborough.*

Presented by Maria J. B. Browne.

THE BRYAN COLLECTION

BYZANTINE SCHOOL.

No.	SUBJECTS OF PAINTINGS.	ARTISTS

176 Virgin and Child.

The Virgin, clothed in a rich crimson drapery which covers the head, holds the infant CHRIST on her right arm. The child has a gilt globe in his hand. Over his head is seen the date of the picture, MXC. It was brought from the East by the celebrated artist, PAPETI, who was sent to Greece by the French Government.

(*Bryan Collection.*)

177. Triptique.

A very remarkable and elaborate work; and of the highest interest in the history of art.

(*Bryan Collection.*)

ITALIAN SCHOOL.

178. A Virgin and Child, with four Saints. *Guido of Sienna.*

This picture is in perfect condition, and is from the renowned collection of M. Artaud de Montor, in the account of which it was engraved. It is described in the work of Gault de St. Germain (p. 51).

(*Bryan Collection.*)

179. Virgin and Child, with Saints. *Cimabue.*

From the De Montor collection—engraved.

(*Bryan Collection.*)

180. Knights at a Tournament. *Giotto di Bodone.*

The frame is as ancient as the picture itself, of which it forms a part. It bears the arms of the Medici family. From the De Montor collection—engraved.

(*Bryan Collection.*)

No. SUBJECTS OF PAINTINGS. ARTISTS

181. Virgin and Child. *Simone Memmi*

The head of the Virgin presents the same type as that exhibited in the portrait of PETRARCH's LAURA, painted by MEMMI, which is in the Library of the Vatican. From the De Montor collection—engraved.

(*Bryan Collection.*)

182. The Last Judgment. *Simone Memmi*

"CHRIST, with the cruciform halo, and the elliptical aureola, bordered with cherubim, appears in the heavens. Above, two angels, strangely enough colored entirely blue, sound the trumpet; below, the Virgin and ST. JOHN kneel upon the ground, from which rises the cross, on which two angels are looking. On the left, the elect, wearing crowns of gold, mount towards the sky, under the protection of a pitying spirit; on the right, the damned, covered with blood, are delivered to the demons by a minister of divine vengeance. JESUS himself wears a terrible expression. MICHAEL ANGELO is, therefore, not the first to have given him this menacing aspect. The general color of the picture pleases the eye by its extreme fineness; the Virgin and ST. JOHN by the beauty of their types." To this just and graphic description from the pen of M. Michiels, which appeared in the *Gazette de France*, it is needless to add anything more. From the De Montor collection.

(*Bryan Collection.*)

183. The Crucifixion. *Taddeo Gaddi.*

From the De Montor collection.

(*Bryan Collection.*)

184. St. Jerome, St. Dominic, and St. Francis of Assisa. *Taddeo Gaddi.*

The three Saints stand side by side. There is dignity in the attitudes and the draperies, and harmony in the color of this picture. From the De Montor collection.

(*Bryan Collection.*)

185. Two Wings of a Tabernacle. *Lorenzo il Monaco.*

From the De Montor collection.

(*Bryan Collection.*)

186. A Tabernacle. *Giottino.*

From the De Montor collection.

(*Bryan Collection.*)

187. St. Anthony. *Giottino.*

From the De Montor collection.

(*Bryan Collection.*)

188 St. Dominic. *Giottino.*

From the De Montor collection.
(Bryan Collection.)

189. Crucifixion. (Half of a Triptique.)
Buonamico Buffalmaco.

From the De Montor collection.
(Bryan Collection.)

190. A Tabernacle. *Buonamico Buffalmaco*

From the De Montor collection.
(Bryan Collection.)

SCHOOL OF THE TWELFTH CENTURY.

191. A Tabernacle.

The carved arabesque work indicates the period of this picture, which has been much injured by the hand of time.

From the De Montor collection.
(Bryan Collection.)

ANCIENT VENETIAN SCHOOL.

192. Virgin adoring the Infant Jesus.

The Virgin kneels before her Divine Son. Around are angels, and behind her is Joseph. Above is a company of angels; and, in the distant sky, one is seen appearing to the shepherds. The infant has a crimson, cruciform aureola. In this rudely-drawn picture the future glory of the Venetian School, its gorgeous color, is plainly indicated.

(Bryan Collection.)

193. The Birth of John the Baptist. *Uccello.*

From the De Montor collection.
(Bryan Collection.)

194. Christ in the Garden of Gethsemane. *Castagno.*

From the De Montor collection.
(Bryan Collection.)

195. Triumph of Julius Cæsar. *Antonio Dello.*

From the De Montor collection.
(Bryan Collection.)

196. The Crucifixion. *Botticelli.*

From the De Montor collection.
(Bryan Collection.)

197. Adoration of the Infant Christ. *Perugino*

The Virgin MARY, ST. JOHN the Baptist, ST. JEROME, ST. JOSEPH, ST. MICHAEL, and the Pope JULIUS II., are kneeling before the divine infant. Three small Angels, also kneeling, carry the nails and the Cross, emblems of the torture which the new-born should suffer. The CHRIST bears a striking resemblance to that of the little JESUS, so much admired, in a painting of the same artist, now placed in the Louvre, after having decorated the gallery of the King of Holland. ST. MICHAEL strikes the beholder by his noble air and his martial type. The head is evidently the portrait of GASTON DE FOIX, the model of the chivalry of the day. ST. JOHN is the lean prophet of the desert, the ascetic, and the eater of locusts and wild honey. At the top of the picture, three Angels play upon different instruments. In the background are seen the Capitol, the image of Roman power, and the vast ruins of the Coliseum. The head of JOSEPH, who stands behind ST. JOHN, must strike the considerate observer by its close resemblance to the type of JOSEPH which we find in the Holy Families of RAPHAEL. In the Cherub who holds the Cross, we also find great similarity to the little Angel who occupies so prominent a position in the famous Madonna of Foglino, from the same divine pencil. From the collection ERRARD. Signed and dated 1509.

(*Bryan Collection.*)

198. St. John, Weeping. *Lionardo da Vinci*

For the authenticity of this picture, we have the high authority of Mr. Woodburn.

(*Bryan Collection.*)

199. St. John. *Lionardo da Vinci*

(*Bryan Collection.*)

200. The Birth and Resurrection of Christ. *Raphael*

In the centre of the upper compartment, CHRIST, draped in red, and bearing the emblematic banner of the Cross, rises from an open tomb. His hand is raised with an expression of command. On each side are two soldiers sleeping, and two starting away in fright. A slender tree also is seen upon each side of the tomb; in the distance is a large hill. In the lower compartment are eight figures, besides the infant CHRIST. Six kneel in a semicircle about the new-born Saviour, who lies in the middle of the foreground. Three of these, on the left, are shepherds. On the right are the Virgin mother and two Angels. Next to MARY sits JOSEPH; and on the extreme left, a fourth shepherd approaches. Two slender trees here also appear on each side of the composition. In the distance are heavily undulating hills.

Very few Raphaels of this period exist. Those which are in the Vatican and the Louvre, show, in style and handling, an exact similarity to these pictures, which is absolutely conclusive. The donor wishes it to be understood, that, in his opinion, and in that of some of the accomplished and practised experts in Europe, there is not the slightest doubt of the authenticity of these pictures. Only the inexperienced and the uncultivated fail to trace in them the pencil of the divine RAPHAEL.

(*Bryan Collection.*)

201. Madonna and Child. *Copy from Raphael*

An old and admirably executed copy of the Bridgewater Madonna.

(*Bryan Collection.*)

202. Dance of Cupids. *Copy from Raphael*

Nine Cupids dance in a ring. On the left, one plays upon double pipes: on the right, another sits upon the ground. This copy is very fine, as it may well be, having been made by no less distinguished an artist than SASSOFERRATO himself.

(*Bryan Collection.*)

203. St. George, and St. Anthony of Padua. *Gaudenzio Ferrari.*

(*Bryan Collection.*)

204. Martyrdom of St. Bartholomew. *Fra Bartolomeo*

(*Bryan Collection.*)

205. The Repose in Egypt. *Giorgione*

No. 192 is a specimen of the ancient Venetian style, which should be examined in connection with these productions of the glorious days of that school.

(*Bryan Collection.*)

206. Prince of Palermo—in Disguise. *Giorgione.*

Similar to that in the Royal Gallery of Naples, it is distinguished by the Prince holding a flute, and not a staff, a ring on his finger and an amulet in his fur cap. From the collection of the Marquis Sommariva.

(*Bryan Collection.*)

207. A Concert. *Copy from Giorgione, by Watteau.*

Two men and a naked female sit in the open air, diverting themselves with music. Another female figure peers at the group from the shrubbery, which is not in the original, but found only in Watteau's Pastiche, No. 423.

(*Bryan Collection.*)

208. The Repose in Egypt. *Titian.*

This composition was repeated many times by TITIAN, and without great variation. This repetition is distinguished by the absence of some figures in the background, and the introduction of a rivulet in the foreground, and a butterfly upon a flower in the right corner. It has twice been found necessary to remove the picture from its canvas: the drapery of the Virgin has suffered somewhat from this and other causes; the other parts of the picture are somewhat injured.

(*Bryan Collection.*)

209. Portrait of a Lady. *Style of Titian.*

From the collection of R. W. Meade, of Philadelphia.

(*Bryan Collection.*)

210. St. Jerome, in his Study. *School of Titian.*

Probably a copy by ODVARDO FIALETTI, scholar of TINTORETTO. This is a large copy of a print by ALBRECHT DURER. Its color shows it evidently to be of the Venetian School.

(*Bryan Collection.*)

211. Virgin and Child. *School of Titian.*

This picture came from the Gallery of Louis Philippe, and on the back was written "*Dans la Chambre du Prince.*"

(*Bryan Collection.*)

212. Portrait of a Presbyter. *Tintoretto.*

(*Bryan Collection.*)

213. St. Benedict. *Francesco Zucco.*

The Saint is prostrate before an altar, receiving the black stole from the Virgin: the head of the Saint is worthy the palette of Titian. Signed and dated. Found in New York, by the donor.

(*Bryan Collection.*)

214. Abraham discarding Hagar and Ishmael. *Paul Veronese.*

(*Bryan Collection.*)

215. Portrait of Charles, Constable de Bourbon. *Ludovico Brea.*

From the collection of General D'Espinoy.

(*Bryan Collection.*)

216. Christ Shown to the Multitude. *Sebastiano del Piombo.*

This picture, which is in very fine condition, and the principal figure in which much resembles that in the famous picture of *Christ looking into Hell*, in the Royal Gallery of Madrid, was purchased by the donor in Rome.

(*Bryan Collection.*)

217. Virgin and Child, with Angels. *Andrea del Sarto.*

(*Bryan Collection.*)

EARLY FLORENTINE SCHOOL.

218. Virgin and Child, with St. John.

It will be noticed that gold is used freely in the halos, and upon the draperies, which fall in somewhat stiff but ample and not unpleasing folds. This picture is from the collection of the Abbe GENOUDE, known as the translator of the Bible, by which he accumulated a fortune.

(*Bryan Collection.*)

219. Adoration of the Shepherds.

This picture is from the collection of the Sylvestre family, and was once improperly attributed to RAPHAEL. It bears many of the marks of GAROFALO's pencil.

(*Bryan Collection.*)

220. The Crucifixion. *Andrea Mantegna.*

Mr. Michiels, the distinguished critic employed by the Belgian Government to prepare a history of Flemish Art, says of this work: "The CHRIST has a nobility in his attitude which few painters have been able to give him; the expression of the good robber is also grave and dignified. The whole picture bears the impress of a serene imagination; the coloring is sombre; the attitudes are distinguished by an air of majesty. We feel that the artist had, at the commencement of his career, severely studied the ancients. Two cuirasses, and some of the draperies, are gilded; gold is mingled with the other costumes, in the form of *traits*, designating the folds. We are particular about these details, because they indicate the primitive epoch in which the picture was painted, and the manner in which they passed from the use of gold grounds to the entire abandonment of that metal."

It should be observed that the Jewish type is preserved in the heads of many of the figures, which is the case of the works of very few other masters. It will be observed that there are in this crowded canvas no two pieces of offensive or defensive armor alike. This is worthy of particular remark, as SQUARCIONI, the master of MANTEGNA, had the largest and most varied collection of ancient arms which existed in his day.

Aside from its intrinsic merit, this picture is of the greatest interest when considered in connection with the *St. Jerome* (222) by CORREGGIO, the disciple of MANTEGNA. In the peculiar mode of introducing gold in the lights of that noble painting, we notice an unmistakable similarity to MANTEGNA's use of the same material in the work before us; thus showing the direct connection between the manner of the two painters.

It is impossible to overrate the historical importance of the juxtaposition of this work of MANTEGNA with that of CORREGGIO. There is afforded in no other gallery, public or private, in the world, a similar opportunity to study the master and scholar side by side in works of unquestionable authenticity and the highest intrinsic merit.

(*Bryan Collection.*)

221. Adoration of the Kings. *Andrea Mantegna.*

Found in Venice, 1859.

(*Bryan Collection.*)

222. The Virgin and Child, Mary Magdalen, and St. Jerome (known as the St. Jerome). *Correggio.*

Of this sketch M. Michiels remarks, that in it "burns in all its grace the talent of CORREGGIO. Never has the ecstacy of piety, or the fervor of religious affection, been better expressed."

This picture differs from the large one at Parma, in the absence of the emblematic lion which stands in that by the side of ST. JEROME; and also in the color of some of the draperies, particularly in that of the canopy, which in this is striped, while in that it is of one color. In this, too, we find gold used in the halos and in the draperies, which is not the case in the other; a fact which points to the earlier production of this picture, and which also connects it in a remarkable manner with the CRUCIFIXION by MANTEGNA (No. 220).

There can be no doubt that this picture is the finished sketch for the well-known *St. Jerome*, at Parma. The marked differences already alluded to in minor points, prove incontestably that it could not be the work of a copyist, who would, of course, reproduce his original with all possible fidelity. It is from the collection of Marshal Sebastiani, it having been nailed firmly to the wall in his bed-chamber.

(*Bryan Collection.*)

223. Virgin and Child. *Correggio.*

In support of the authenticity of this picture, we have the first authority in England,—that of Mr. Woodburn. The donor thinks it may be SCHIDONE.

(*Bryan Collection.*)

224. Virgin and Child. *Bernardino Lovini.*

(*Bryan Collection.*)

225. Virgin and Child, with St. John. *Giulio Romano.*

This picture was attributed to CESARE DA SESTO, but is now believed by the donor to be by GIULIO ROMANO. It is from the collection of Bishop Luscomb, Paris.

(*Bryan Collection.*)

226. Portrait of a Princess of Florence. *Agnolo Bronzino.*

(Bryan Collection.)

227. Portrait of a Noble Florentine as St. Barbe. *Agnolo Bronzino.*

(Bryan Collection.)

228. Portrait of a Venetian Lady as Mary Magdalen. *Copy from Palma (Vecchio).*

(Bryan Collection.)

229. Charity. *Giuseppe Cesari d'Arpinas.*

(Bryan Collection.)

230. Virgin and Child. *Annibale Caracci.*

(Bryan Collection.)

231. St. Joseph holding the Infant Jesus. *Annibale Caracci.*

(Bryan Collection.)

232. St. Paul borne to Heaven by Angels. *Domenichino.*

"Three angels bear aloft the interpreter of the divine will: one has the form of infancy, another of youth, the third of adolescence. The minister of our Lord raises his hands to heaven, on which he gazes with an expression of burning hope. How he seeks to discover the first rays of the eternal light! How he longs for the moment in which he shall appear before the Almighty! What enthusiasm animates his countenance! I doubt if the ardor of faith could be better shown. The little angel has those brilliant eyes, and that expressive visage, which this master knew so well how to paint; it is certainly not inferior to those which we admire in the grand saloon of the Louvre. The angel of the second age charms the eye by a grace and an easiness of attitude extremely remarkable; upon his countenance burn the veneration and the love with which the Apostle inspires him. The entire group seems actually to mount in the air. Mr. Bryan had the good taste to purchase it at the sale of M. Forbin-Janson."

To this just and graphic description, from the pen of M. Michiels, which appeared in the *Gazette de France*, it is needless to add anything more.

This picture was formerly in the gallery of the Cardinal Lambruschini, and afterwards in the collection of M. Forbin-Janson, Director of the Louvre, at whose sale it was purchased by the donor.

(Bryan Collection.)

233. Christ Crowned with Thorns. *Guido*

If not original, it is the best copy ever seen by the donor.

(Bryan Collection.)

No.	SUBJECTS OF PAINTINGS.	ARTISTS
234.	Magdalen in a Trance.	*School of Guido.*

This picture is from the collection of Louis Philippe. The head of the Magdalen is evidently a reminiscence of the Niobe discovered at Rome at the epoch of the painter.

(Bryan Collection.)

235. The Young Bacchus. *School of Carlo Dolci.*

(Bryan Collection.)

236. Lucretia. *School of Carlo Dolci.*

(Bryan Collection.)

237. Magdalen. *School of Carlo Dolci.*

(Bryan Collection.)

238. St. Dorothea. *School of Carlo Dolci.*

(Bryan Collection.)

239. Christ disputing with the Doctors. *Gentileschi.*

(Bryan Collection.)

240. Portrait of Galileo Galilei. *Justus Sustermans.*

From the collection of Louis Philippe.

(Bryan Collection.)

241. Virgin and Child. *Sassoferrato.*

Found at Rome.

(Bryan Collection.)

242. Landscape, with Historical Figures. *Salvator Rosa.*

(Bryan Collection.)

243. Landscape. *School of Salvator Rosa.*

(Bryan Collection.)

244. Landscape. *School of Salvator Rosa.*

(Bryan Collection.)

245. Landscape. *School of Salvator Rosa.*

(Bryan Collection.)

246. Marine View, with Architecture. *Canaletto.*

Figures by Tiepolo.

(Bryan Collection.)

247. Autumn. *Artist Unknown.*

Purchased of Mr. Terry, artist, Rome.

(Bryan Collection.)

248. Philip IV. of Spain.

Bought at Sienna.
(*Bryan Collection.*)

249. Don John of Austria.

Bought at Sienna.
(*Bryan Collection.*)

250. A Theologian Decorated with the Order of the Golden Fleece.

Bought at Sienna.
(*Bryan Collection.*)

251. Portrait.

Bought at Sienna.
(*Bryan Collection.*)

252. Portrait.

Bought at Sienna.
(*Bryan Collection.*)

FLEMISH AND DUTCH SCHOOLS.

253. A Landscape. *Jacques van Artois*

From the collection of Marshal Oudinot.
(*Bryan Collection.*)

254. Landscape. *Jan Asselyn.*

(*Bryan Collection.*)

255. Landscape. *School of Asselyn.*

(*Bryan Collection.*)

256. Marine View. *Ludolf Bakhuysen.*

(*Bryan Collection.*)

257. A large Marine View. *School of Bakhuysen.*

(*Bryan Collection.*)

258. Marine View. *School of Bakhuysen.*

(*Bryan Collection.*)

259. Winter Scene. *Jan Beerestraten.*

This is the finest specimen of the Master ever seen by the donor. It graced the collection of Cardinal Fesch.
(*Bryan Collection.*)

260. Boors Regaling. *Cornelius Bega.*

(*Bryan Collection.*)

261. Landscape. *Thierry van Bergen.*

This is not a remarkable, though it is an authentic, specimen of the Master, and is signed.

(*Bryan Collection.*)

262. Italian Scenery, and Figures in Italian Costume. *Nicholas Berghem.*

Dated and signed "BERCHEM," his true signature, and a superb specimen of this Master.

(*Bryan Collection.*)

263. Landscape, with Oxen at the plough. *Copy of Nicholas Berghem.*

This picture was considered a BERGHEM by the Comte de Turenne, in the catalogue of his collection.

(*Bryan Collection.*)

264. Cattle and Herdsmen. *Nicholas Berghem.*

This little picture, though much injured, is unquestionably authentic.

(*Bryan Collection.*)

265. Cattle Market. *Petrus van Bloemen.*

The ruined buildings near which the cattle are grouped, are the remains of the Palace of the Cæsars, Rome.

(*Bryan Collection.*)

266. Halt of Soldiers. *Petrus van Bloemen.*

These two pictures were engraved as the works of DE LAER, by an English engraver, in 1769; an error of names but not of appreciation at that time, when DE LAER was rated with WOUVERMANS.

(*Bryan Collection.*)

267. Halt of Cavaliers. *Petrus van Bloemen.*

This is in his Flemish style.

(*Bryan Collection.*)

268. Landscape. *Jan Both.*

(*Bryan Collection.*)

269. Landscape. *Jan Both.*

(*Bryan Collection.*)

270. Italian Landscape: Sunrise. *Jan Both.*

(*Bryan Collection.*)

271. Italian Landscape: Sunset. *Jan Both.*

270 and 271 are companion pictures: the spirited figures are by LINGELBACH.

(Bryan Collection.)

272. Interior of a Tavern. *Richard Brakenburg.*

It is signed both by BRAKENBURG and JAN STEEN, and bears everywhere marks of the careful assistance of the latter.

(Bryan Collection.)

273. A Presentation to the Temple. *Leonard Bramer*

Signed and dated. Bought from J. Vollmering in New York city. It is as fine as REMBRANDT's best works. The senior of REMBRANDT, he appears to have led the way for him in his shades.

(Bryan Collection.)

274. Robber examining Coin by Day-light. *Adrian Brower.*

This Master was much respected by RUBENS.

(Bryan Collection.)

275. Robber examining Coin by Candle-light. *Adrian Brower.*

(Bryan Collection.)

276. Portrait of a Jansenist. *Phillippe de Champagne.*

This picture is an excellent specimen of the Master. Collection of Mr. VIEN, artist.

(Bryan Collection.)

277. St. Paul. *Phillippe de Champagne.*

(Bryan Collection.)

278 Cattle in a Landscape. *Albert Klomp.*

(Bryan Collection.)

279. An Equestrian Portrait. *Gonzales de Coques.*

The picture gives but a feeble idea of the merit of the painter.

(Bryan Collection.)

280. Cattle and Figures in a Landscape. *Albert Cuyp*

(Bryan Collection.)

296\. The Marriage of St. Catherine. *Jan Hemling.*

The picture is in remarkably fine condition, and, aside from its intrinsic merit, is important in the history of Art. When purchased by the donor, its beauties were hidden beneath the accumulated blackness of ages; otherwise a private American fortune would have failed to obtain it, as the Director of the National Academy of Brussels, partly suspecting its value, was a competitor for its possession. It was purchased at the sale of the well-known *Collection Quedeville.*

(*Bryan Collection.*)

297\. The Annunciation. *Copy from Jan Hemling*

This picture, as well as the preceding, is from the *Collection Quedeville*, and was supposed, for a long time, by some, to be an original; but a comparison of it with the "Marriage of St. Catherine," just noticed, will soon convince even the least practised eye of the error of this belief.

(*Bryan Collection.*)

298\. A Triptique. *Early Flemish School.*

Virgin and child beneath a canopy surrounded by angels offering music and gifts.

(*Bryan Collection.*)

299\. View of an old City on the Rhine. *Jan van der Heyde.*

(*Bryan Collection.*)

300\. Landscape. *School of Mindert Hobbema.*

(*Bryan Collection.*)

301\. A Landscape. *Cornelius Huysmans, of Malines.*

This is the finest easel-picture of this Master known to the donor. One inferior to it in every respect was placed by the side of a HOBBEMA at the exhibition of the British Institution, 1851, and sustained itself.

(*Bryan Collection.*)

302\. Portrait. *Karl du Jardin.*

Portraits by this Master are very rare.

(*Bryan Collection.*)

303\. Landscape, with Figures. *Karl du Jardin.*

The signature is in script, *K. du Jardin;* an unusual one for the Master, who almost always signed in Roman letters.

(*Bryan Collection.*)

No.	SUBJECTS OF PAINTINGS.	ARTISTS

304. Landscape: Cattle and Figures. *Jan Kobell.*

Purchased in New York city.
(*Bryan Collection.*)

305. Portrait. *Sir Peter Lely.*

This is the portrait of a sister to the Duke whose portrait, representing him holding an orange, is in the Louvre, and which was long attributed to VANDYKE; and the donor, with due deference, declares both portraits to be painted by the same artist—Sir PETER LELY. It is from the collection of DROLLING, artist.

(*Bryan Collection.*)

306. Portrait. *Nicholas Maas.*

(*Bryan Collection.*)

307. Virgin and Child, with Cherubs. *Jan de Mabuse.*

(*Bryan Collection.*)

308. Virgin and Child. *Jan de Mabuse.*

This picture in its composition and expression shows the influence of the painter's study in Italy.

(*Bryan Collection.*)

309. A Triptique. *Quintin Matsys.*

Bodily rather than mental suffering is portrayed in this picture by a painter who sought expression alone. His Misers, in the English Queen's collection, is the connecting link between the early and the more modern Flemish art.

(*Bryan Collection.*)

310. Boors regaling. *Jan Molenaer.*

(*Bryan Collection.*)

311. Winter Scene. *Nicholas Molenaer*

(*Bryan Collection.*)

312. Landscape. *Frederic Moucheron.*

This picture is signed by the artist.

(*Bryan Collection.*)

313. Landscape. *Frederic Moucheron.*

Bought in New York city.
(*Bryan Collection.*)

314. Portrait. *Jan van Neck*

This picture is from the gallery of Cardinal Fesch, at the sale of which it was purchased,—but not by the donor,—as by NETSCHER, the true signature being covered by the false one of NETSCHER.

(*Bryan Collection.*)

to have painted on cedar panel. It formed one compartment of a triptique in the Cathedral of Antwerp. The centre compartment represented the Flagellation of Christ.

The donor has the authority of Mr. Heris for the authenticity of this picture, and the locality from which it was stolen.

(Bryan Collection.)

336. Portrait of a Knight of the Order of the Golden Fleece. *Peter Paul Rubens.*

This picture is from the collection of Louis Philippe, King of the French, and was supposed to be by Vandyke.

(Bryan Collection.)

337 Hercules strangling the Nemean Lion. *Peter Paul Rubens.*

Several persons, whose opinions the donor highly respects, have denied the authenticity of this picture; but he thinks that, on a careful examination, its wonderful energy and muscular movement can be attributed to no other hand, no other head, than that of Rubens. It is the Belvidere Torso—that only acknowledged Master of Michael Angelo—put into action, and was doubtless painted in Italy. It is known that Rubens attempted to draw the lion from nature, when he was irritated by his keeper. He made but a hasty sketch.

(Bryan Collection.)

338. Landscape, with Figures. *Peter Paul Rubens*

From an old chateau in Normandy.

(Bryan Collsction.)

339. Ascension of the Virgin. *Copy from Peter Paul Rubens.*

This copy was made by Cornelius Poelemburg.

(Bryan Collection.)

340. Group of Christ, St. John, and two Angels. *Copy from Peter Paul Rubens.*

(Bryan Collection.)

341. Satyr and Nymphs. *School of Rubens*

(Bryan Collection.)

342. Effect of Candle-light. *School of Rubens.*

Copied from a well-known etching of Rubens.

(Bryan Collection.)

343. Distant View of Haarlem. *Jacob Ruysdael*

The figures in the foreground are by VANDERVELDE.

(*Bryan Collection.*)

344. Marine View. *Jacob Ruysdael.*

The figures are by VANDERVELDE.

(*Bryan Collection.*)

345. Landscape, with Cattle. *School of Ruysdael.*

(*Bryan Collection.*)

346. Landscape. *Solomon Ruysdael.*

(*Bryan Collection.*)

347. Dogs Worrying a Cat. *Francis Snyders.*

The landscape by WILDENS, the cat by OUDRY, by whom it was added, and to whom the picture belonged. From the collection of DROLLING the artist.

(*Bryan Collection.*)

348. Still Life. *Francis Snyders.*

Collection of Marshal Oudinot.

(*Bryan Collection.*)

349. Interior: Family Scene. *Jan Steen.*

The patient is the painter's own wife; on the right are the VAN GOYENS, (her father and mother,) and JAN STEEN himself stands on her left hand, regarding the operation with interest.

This picture, which is superior to the only specimen of the Master in the Louvre, was purchased from the Gallery of the Count De Turenne, the last of the family of the celebrated Marshal.

(*Bryan Collection.*)

350 Landscape and Figures. *Jan Steen.*

Signed by the artist, and bought in New York city.

(*Bryan Collection.*)

351 Incantation Scene. *David Teniers the Younger*

This picture is unsurpassed by any other of the Master; and if ever equalled, it is only by one in the Gallery of Madrid, representing TENIERS himself, painting the portrait of the Grand Duke Leopold and his family; a picture which makes painters wonder and despair. Collection Sylvestre.

(*Bryan Collection.*)

368. The Burning and Sacking of a Town.

Philip Wouvermans.

If not a copy, it is an early picture of the Master, and though meritorious, gives no idea of the fullness of his powers.

(Bryan Collection.)

369. Landscape. *Jan Wynants.*

The equestrians and beggar in the foreground are by Barent Gaal. It is a fair specimen of the Master. Collection Giroud, Paris.

(Bryan Collection.)

370. Still Life. *Henry Martin Rokes.*

It, as well as the "Sorcery Scene," by Teniers, ornamented the collection of Mons. Sylvestre, whose ancestors have been either artists or connected with art since the year 1490. A noble pedigree. This artist inherited the name of *Zorg* (careful) from his father.

(Bryan Collection.)

371. Ruins, with Figures. *Flemish School.*

(Bryan Collection.)

GERMAN SCHOOL.

372. Venus and Cupid. *Lucas Cranach.*

(Bryan Collection.)

373. Portrait of a Lady. *Lucas Cranach.*

It is from this painter's pencil that we have the only known or recognized portrait of Martin Luther. Collection D'Espinoy.

(Bryan Collection.)

374. Portrait. *Balthazar Denner.*

An old Lady, with a silk hood. The marks of age are given with great accuracy and truthfulness.

(Bryan Collection.)

375. St. George and the Dragon. *Albert Durer.*

(Bryan Collection.)

376. Triumph of Christianity. *School of Durer*

This picture is from the collection Quedeville.

(Bryan Collection.)

377. Interior of a Private Chapel. *Hans Holbein.*

The family of Count Valkeniers are at prayers—the father and the two eldest sons being in armor, ready to depart for war.

From the collection of Joseph M. Meert de Domberg, New York.

(*Bryan Collection.*)

378. Portrait of a Professor. *Hans Holbein.*

(*Bryan Collection.*)

379. The Judgment of Paris. *Joachim Uytenwael.*

(*Bryan Collection.*)

380. Adoration. *Martin Schoen.*

On the right will be seen a Priest, holding a book, and supposed, by General D'Espinoy, from whose collection it came, to be a portrait of Luther, in his youth.

(*Bryan Collection.*)

381. **Landscape, with** Figures. *Valkenburg*

(*Bryan Collection.*)

382. Landscape. *Valkenburg*

These pictures possess great interest, in being historically known as the earliest landscapes painted otherwise than as a mere accessory to some historical, religious, or other subject. Both of them are from the collection Quedeville.

(*Bryan Collection.*)

SPANISH SCHOOL.

383. Philip IV. of Spain, as David with Goliath's Head. *Diego Velasquez*

From the collection of Marshal Sebastiani.

(*Bryan Collection.*)

384. Landscape. *Diego Velasquez*

Found at Rome. A picture of a similar style—the only one ever seen by the donor—is in the possession of Mr. Madrazo, the Director of the Royal Gallery of Madrid.

(*Bryan Collection.*)

385. Portrait of the Infanta Margarita of Spain. *Diego Velasquez*

From the collection of R. W. Meade, U. S. Consul at Cadiz. 1808.

(*Bryan Collection.*)

402. Portrait of Duchesnois, the Flemish Sculptor. *Nicholas Poussin.*

Duchesnois lived with POUSSIN in Rome. From the collection of Gen. D'Espinoy.

(*Bryan Collection.*)

403. Landscape. *Guaspre Poussin.*

(*Bryan Collection.*)

404. Landscape. *Guaspre Poussin*

(*Bryan Collection.*)

405. Grand Landscape: Hagar in the Desert. *Guaspre Poussin.*

This picture, which has been engraved, is in the finest manner of the Master. The figures are by PHILIPPE LAURI. It is from the collection of Marshal Sebastiani.

(*Bryan Collection.*)

406. Landscape, with Figures. *School of Claude Lorraine.*

The peasants in the foreground are designed after DOMENICHINO; but the figure who leans against a tree, in the shadow on the left, and plays upon a pipe, is like CLAUDE. CLAUDE was so conscious of the want of merit in his pictures, he used to say that he sold his landscapes and gave away the people in them. Collection of Marshal Sebastiani.

(*Bryan Collection.*)

407. A Grand Landscape, Marine View, and Figures, an Ancient Group in marble representing Echo punished. *School of Claude Lorraine.*

This picture belonged to M. Forbin-Janson, Director of the Louvre; it was believed by him to be an original.

(*Bryan Collection.*)

408. Landscape, with a Sea-View. *School of Claude Lorraine.*

(*Bryan Collection.*)

409. Landscape. *School of Claude Lorraine*

(*Bryan Collection.*)

No.	SUBJECTS OF PAINTINGS.	ARTISTS
410.	Portrait of a Lady at her Toilet. (*Bryan Collection.*)	*Pierre Mignard*
411.	Holy Family. (*Bryan Collection.*)	*Pierre Mignard.*
412.	The dead Christ supported by the Virgin. From the collection of the Abbe Genoud. (*Bryan Collection.*)	*Eustache le Sueur.*
413.	Portrait. From the Parant Collection. (*Bryan Collection.*)	*Charles le Brun.*
414.	Battle-Piece. (*Bryan Collection.*)	*Jacques Courtois.*
415.	Battle-Piece. (*Bryan Collection.*)	*Jacques Courtois.*
416.	Christ in the Wilderness, ministered to by Angels. This picture was formerly in the collection of Cardinal Fesch. After its arrival in Paris, in the possession of the donor, it was solicited for the Gallery of the Louvre. (*Bryan Collection.*)	*Charles de la Fosse.*
417. 418.	Scenes from the Life of St. Charles de Borromeo. (*Bryan Collection.*)	*Jean Jouvenet.*
419.	Portraits of two Ladies. This picture was also sought from the donor for the Gallery of the Louvre. (*Bryan Collection.*)	*Nicholas de Largilliere.*
420.	**Portrait of a** Marshal of France. From the Collection Vien. It is a very fine specimen of the Master. Our own STUART thought the Portraits of RIGAUD's two sisters, by him, the most natural and true he ever saw. (*Bryan Collection.*)	*Hyacinthe Rigaud*

421. Musicians. *Antoine Watteau.*

This picture is evidently cut from a large and important work.

(*Bryan Collection.*)

422. A Venetian Fête, or Ball, by day. *Antoine Watteau*

A composition unrivalled for picturesqueness of design and richness of color.

(*Bryan Collection.*)

423. Landscape, with Figures. *Antoine Watteau.*

This is but a sketch, in the style of GIORGIONE. (See No. 207.)

(*Bryan Collection.*)

424. Landscape, with Figures. *Jean Baptiste Pater.*

(*Bryan Collection.*)

425. Portrait of the Cardinal de Rochechouart. *Pompeo Battoni.*

From the Chateau Courcelle, the seat of the Cardinal's family.

(*Bryan Collection.*)

426. Head of a Boy. *Pompeo Battoni.*

(*Bryan Collection.*)

427. Still Life. *Jean B. S. Chardin.*

The viands for a *jour maigre* under the rule of the Church.

(*Bryan Collection.*)

428. Portrait of Louis XVII., Dauphin. *School of Greuze.*

He is represented as seven or eight years old. He wears a blue scarf indicating his rank. From the collection of M. de Mont Louis, a devoted legitimist, who died at a very advanced age, in 1850. It bears much resemblance to the works of CHARDIN.

(*Bryan Collection.*)

429. Park of St. Cloud. *Hubert Robert.*

(*Bryan Collection.*)

430 Portrait of Dr. Ambroise Paré, the Father of French Surgery. *Peter Porbus.*

(*Bryan Collection.*)

431. Italian Scenery, with Figures. *Joseph Vernet.*

Painted by the artist for his friend, Balthazar, the architect, from whose collection it ca s. It is a fair specimen of the Master.

(Bryan Collection.)

432. The Bay of Baia, an effect of Moonlight. *Joseph Vernet.*

(Bryan Collection.)

433. A Seaport. *Joseph Vernet.*

(Bryan Collection.)

434. Landscape, painted for a Snuff-Box. *Joseph Vernet.*

(Bryan Collection.)

435. Portrait of a Receiver-General. *Robert Tourniere.*

(Bryan Collection.)

436. A Nymph of Diana. *Jean Baptiste Greuze.*

437. A Repetition of the L'Aveugle Trompé. *Jean Baptiste Greuze.*

An early production. Bought in New York city.

(Bryan Collection.)

438. Portrait of the Duc de Choiseul. *Jean Baptiste Greuze.*

From the collection of PARANT, who painted, on porcelain, the heads of the celebrities of France. This head was probably procured for that purpose.

(Bryan Collection.)

439. Head of a Young Girl. *Jean Baptiste Greuze.*

(Bryan Collection.)

440. Virginie. (A study.) *Jean Baptiste Greuze.*

(Bryan Collection.)

441. Sketch of a Female Head. *Jean Baptiste Greuze.*

The celebrated miniature-painter SAINT purchased this sketch at the sale of GREUZE's own collection after his death.

(Bryan Collection.)

442. The Sister. *Nicholas Bernard Lepicié.*

(*Bryan Collection.*)

443. France Triumphant after the Restoration of Louis XVIII. *Pierre Paul Prud'hon*

This picture is the finished sketch of a plafond now at Dijon, the birth-place of the painter. It is from the collection of M. VIEN, artist. It was sought of the donor by the Director of the Louvre, for that Gallery.

(*Bryan Collection.*)

444. Napoleon at Charleroi. *Horace Vernet*

The accessories and the horse are portraits. This little picture ornamented the private study of Louis Philippe.

(*Bryan Collection.*)

445. The Duke of Orleans. *Horace Vernet*

The Duke is giving orders to his groom. He is attended by a negro-page and two greyhounds. In the background are a "cabriolet" and horse. This is a very early picture of the Master. It was rescued from the Chateau and Park de Monceau, on their destruction.

(*Bryan Collection.*)

446. Attack repulsed at Constantine, Africa. *Bellangé.*

Death of Richepanse.

(*Bryan Collection.*)

447. Fox-Chase. *J. B. Decamps*

(*Bryan Collection.*)

448. Snipe-Shooting. *J. B. Decamps*

(*Bryan Collection.*)

449. Duck-Shooting. *J. B. Decamps.*

(*Bryan Collection.*)

450. Nymphs and Cupids. *Vallin.*

(*Bryan Collection.*)

451 Portrait of a Lady, as a Water-Nymph. *Schaal.*

It has been engraved as LA BELLE SOURCE, and is supposed to be the portrait of the wife of a revolutionary character of some note, named Source. From the Collection PARANT.

(*Bryan Collection.*)

452. A Voluptuary. *François Boucher*

(*Bryan Collection.*)

No.	SUBJECTS OF PAINTINGS.	ARTISTS

453. Winter-Scene. *François Boucher.*

(*Bryan Collection.*)

454. Landscape. *Georges Michel.*

The figures, by Swebach, are very spirited.

(*Bryan Collection.*)

455. Landscape. *Frederic M. Kruseman.*

(*Bryan Collection.*)

456. The Inheritance. *Felix Van der Eycken.*

Painted for the donor.

(*Bryan Collection.*)

457. Student Travellers, regaling at a Hostelry in Flanders. *Felix Van der Eycken.*

Bought in New York city.

(*Bryan Collection.*)

458. Landscape, with Sheep. *Balthasar Ommeganck.*

(*Bryan Collection.*)

459. Catechism before Marriage, according to Belgian Law, being necessary for State and Matrimonial Security. *Jean Henri de Coene.*

(*Bryan Collection.*)

460. Portrait of an Old Man. *M. Dykemans.*

(*Bryan Collection.*)

461. Portrait of the Artist. *John Singleton Copley.*

(*Bryan Collection.*)

462. Portrait of Guy Bryan. *Thomas Sully.*

This portrait was considered by Dunlap one of the happiest efforts of Mr. Sully.

(*Bryan Collection.*)

463. The Confessional. *William West.*

Mr. West is well known by his having painted the best portrait of Lord Byron. This picture was a favorite of the late Washington Irving.

(*Bryan Collection.*)

464. Landscape. *George L. Brown*

This view is from Nature, in the Island of Capri, Vesuvius being seen in the distance.

(*Bryan Collection.*)

465. A Midnight Conversation. *William Hogarth*

Engraved as the frontispiece of Ireland's Hogarth. In Walpole's anecdotes of painters a catalogue is given professing to contain a complete list of all of HOGARTH's paintings and their then owners. This painting appears in that list, but the owner's name is not given.

(*Bryan Collection.*)

466. The Harlot's Progress.

Copy from William Hogarth.

This copy is by HORREMANS, of Vienna, and is one of the famous series of the "Harlot's Progress." The copyist has seen fit to make some variations from the print.

(*Bryan Collection.*)

467 Portrait. *Sir Joshua Reynolds.*

In his early style.

(*Bryan Collection.*)

468. Pallas appearing to Achilles, after the death of Patroclus. *Benjamin West.*

This is a sketch for a large picture.

(*Bryan Collection.*)

469. Portrait of Charles Wilson Peale. *Benjamin West.*

(*Bryan Collection.*)

470. View of Genesee Falls, New York.

Count Beaujolais.

This sketch is quite faithful as a representation of the locality. Its chief interest, however, consists in its having been made by the brother of Louis Philippe, when the two princes were on their visit to this country, after the first French Revolution. Collection Louis Philippe.

(*Bryan Collection.*)

471. Landscape. *Joseph Vollmering.*

(*Bryan Collection.*)

472. Winter-Scene. *Joseph Vollmering*

(*Bryan Collection.*)

473 Murillo sketching the Beggar-Boy. *Edwin White.*

(*Bryan Collection.*)

474. Family Group. *Charles Wilson* **Peale**

This composition contains portraits of the artist and his family, Major David Ramsey, the historian, and the old dog Argus, so well known to the frequenters of the Museum. The following inscription is on the picture: "C. W. Peale painted these portraits of his family in 1773—wishing to finish every work he had undertaken—completed this picture in 1809."

(*Bryan Collection.*)

475. Portrait of George Washington. *Charles Wilson Peale.*

(*Bryan Collection.*)

476. Portrait of John Beale Bordley. *Charles Wilson Peale.*

(*Bryan Collection.*)

477. Portrait of Pieter Johan Van Berckel. *Charles Wilson Peale.*

Minister Plenipotentiary from the Netherlands to the United States of America, 1782—being the first Minister sent and recognized.

(*Bryan Collection.*)

478. Portrait of Gilbert C. Stuart. *Charles Wilson and Rembrandt Peale.*

(*Bryan Collection.*)

479. Portrait of George Washington. *Gilbert C. Stuart.*

(*Bryan Collection.*)

480. Portrait of John Adams. *Gilbert C. Stuart*

(*Bryan Collection.*)

481. Portrait of Alexander Hamilton.

(*Bryan Collection.*)

482. Portrait of Thomas Jefferson. *Rembrandt Peale*

(*Bryan Collection.*)

No.	SUBJECTS OF PAINTINGS.	ARTISTS
483.	Portrait of Dr. Joseph Priestley. (*Bryan Collection.*)	*Rembrandt Peale.*
484.	Portrait of Mrs. James Madison. (*Bryan Collection.*)	*Rembrandt Peale*
485.	Portrait of Stephen Decatur, U. S. N. (*Bryan Collection.*)	*Rembrandt Peale.*
486.	Portrait of Jacob Jones, U. S. N. (*Bryan Collection.*)	*Rembrandt Peale.*
487.	Portrait of William Bainbridge, U. S. N. (*Bryan Collection.*)	*Rembrandt Peale.*
488.	Portrait of Oliver H. Perry, U. S. N. (*Bryan Collection.*)	*Rembrandt Peale.*
489.	Portrait of William Handy, M. D. (*Bryan Collection.*)	*Edward Savage.*
490.	Portrait of the Seneca Chief, Corn Plant, or Ki-on-twog-ky. This portrait was painted at New York city, in the year 1796, and is engraved in McKenney's History of the Indian Tribes, Vol. I., page 85. (*Bryan Collection.*)	*F. Bartoli*
491.	Portrait of Jean Parisot de la Valette. Grand Master of the Knights of Malta, 1565. A modern copy of this picture is in the Gallery at Versailles. (*Bryan Collection.*)	
492.	Portrait of Cadwallader D. Colden. (*Bryan Collection.*)	*John Wesley Jarvis*

No.	SUBJECTS OF PAINTINGS	ARTISTS
493	Portrait of William Tilghman. Chief Justice of Pennsylvania. (*Bryan Collection.*)	*Rembrandt Peale.*
494.	A Presentation at the Temple. (*Bryan Collection.*)	*Spanish School*
495.	St. Cecilia. In the Style of CORREGGIO. (*Bryan Collection.*)	
496.	Fête Champêtre. (*Bryan Collection.*)	*Gonzales de Coques.*
497.	Female Head. (*Bryan Collection.*)	*School of Correggio.*
498.	St. Paul restored to Sight. (*Bryan Collection.*)	*Copy from Domenichino.*
499.	Adoration of the Shepherds. (*Bryan Collection.*)	*Copy from Spagnoletto.*
500.	Female Head. Original in the Lichtenstein Gallery. (*Bryan Collection.*)	*Copy from Greuze.*
501.	Family Group, of the Artist, Wife and Children. (*Bryan Collection.*)	*Michael Van Musscher.*
502.	Æneas and his son Ascanius visiting Dido. (*Bryan Collection.*)	*Constantine Netscher.*
503.	Portrait of Orelia Doria. (*Bryan Collection.*)	*Italian School.*
504.	Portrait of Madalena Doria. (*Bryan Collection.*)	*Italian School.*
505.	German Baron and his Family. (*Bryan Collection.*)	*Bartholomew Vander Helst.*
506.	Virgin and Child. (*Bryan Collection.*)	

NO.	SUBJECTS OF PAINTINGS.	ARTISTS
507.	Christ appearing to the Magdalen. (Bryan Collection.)	*Fra Bartolomeo*
508.	Virgin and Child. (Bryan Collection.)	*Bernardo Zenale.*
509.	Triptique. (Bryan Collection.)	
510.	Landscape, with Figures. (Bryan Collection.)	*Adam Pynaker.*
511.	Family Fête. (Bryan Collection.)	*Jan Steen.*
512.	Landscape, with Figures. (Bryan Collection.)	*William de Buytenweg.*
513.	Bacchanal. (Bryan Collection.)	*Sebastien Bourdon.*
514.	Landscape, with Figures. (Bryan Collection.)	*Cornelius Huysmans*
515.	Landscape. (Bryan Collection.)	*Minderhout Hobbema.*
516.	The Fortune Teller. (Bryan Collection.)	*Antoine Watteau.*
517.	Snow Scene. (Bryan Collection.)	*Philip Wouverman.*
518.	Dutch Interior. (Bryan Collection.)	*Renier Brakenburg.*
519.	Portrait of Margerethea De Bije. (Bryan Collection.)	*Constantine Netscher.*
520.	Interior of a Cottage. (Bryan Collection.)	
521.	Portrait of a Dog. (Bryan Collection.)	*John B. Weenix.*
522.	The Artist. (Bryan Collection.)	*Godfrey Schalcken.*
523.	Landscape with Cattle. (Bryan Collection.)	*Albert Cuyp.*

No.	SUBJECTS OF PAINTINGS.	ARTISTS.
524.	Italian Landscape. (Bryan Collection.)	*John Hakkert.*
525.	Still Life. (Bryan Collection.)	*J. B. Simeon Chardin.*
526.	The Sacrifice. (Bryan Collection.)	*Leonard Bramer.*
527.	The Village Fête. (Bryan Collection.)	*Renier Brakenburg.*
528.	Flemish Interior. (Bryan Collection.)	*Renier Brakenburg*
529.	Portrait. (Bryan Collection.)	*J. B. Simeon Chardin*
530.	Landscape. (Bryan Collection.)	*Adam Pynaker.*
531.	Pleasure Party. (Bryan Collection.)	*Antoine Watteau.*
532.	Interior. (Bryan Collection.)	*Egbert van Heemskerk.*
533.	The Virgin and the Infant Jesus crushing the Serpent. (Bryan Collection.)	*Pietro Berretini da Cortona.*
534.	Landscape. (Bryan Collection.)	*Dutch School.*
535.	Entrance to a Park. (Bryan Collection.)	*Isaac Moucheron and John Lingelbach.*
536.	Marine View. (Bryan Collection.)	
537.	Portrait. (Bryan Collection.)	*Francis Hals*
538.	Winter Scene. (Bryan Collection.)	*Egbert Vander Poel.*
539.	Portrait. (Bryan Collection.)	*Mlle. Ledoux*

NO.	SUBJECTS OF PAINTINGS.	ARTISTS.
540.	Landscape. (Bryan Collection.)	*Isaac Moucheron.*
541.	Portrait of a Gentleman. (Bryan Collection.)	*Gerard Terburg.*
542.	Portrait of a Lady. (Bryan Collection.)	*Gerard Terburg.*
543.	Temptation of St. Anthony. (Bryan Collection.)	*Matthew Van Hellemont.*
544.	The Frozen Canal. (Bryan Collection.)	*Hendrik Van Avercamp.*
545.	Portrait of a Lady. (Bryan Collection.)	*Thomas Gainsborough.*
546.	Landscape. (Bryan Collection.)	*Adam Pynaker.*
547.	The Lovers. (Bryan Collection.)	
548.	Interior. (Bryan Collection.)	*Adrian Van Ostade.*
549.	St. Jerome at Prayer. (Bryan Collection.)	*Lodovico Mazzolino.*
550.	Family Group. (Bryan Collection.)	*Henry Goltzius.*
551.	Virgin and Child. (Bryan Collection.)	
552.	The Flight into Egypt. (Bryan Collection.)	
553.	Virgin and Child. (Bryan Collection.)	*Bernard Van Orley.*
554.	Scene from "M. de Pourceaugnac." (Bryan Collection.)	*Antoine Watteau.*
555.	The Fatigues of War. (Bryan Collection.)	*Antoine Watteau.*
556.	The Relaxations of War. (Bryan Collection.)	*Antoine Watteau.*

No.	SUBJECTS OF PAINTINGS.	ARTISTS

557 Portrait of William L. Stone. (25×30.)
Edward D. Marchant.

Presented by John B. Hall.

558. Portrait of William Johnson, 1819. (25¾ ×31½.) *John Wesley Jarvis.*

Presented by Horace Binney, Jr.

559. } Views of Niagara Falls. (29×168½.)
560. } *John Trumbull.*

Presented by Dr. Alexander E. Hosack.

561. Portrait of Fitz-Greene Halleck, 1831. (3½ ×5.) Pencil drawing. *Henry Inman.*

Presented by Mrs. Charles A. Davis.

562. Portrait of James Madison. (20×24.)
A. B. Durand.

Presented by P. Kemble Paulding.

563. Portrait of George W. Bethune, D.D. (25 ×30.) Oval. *Rembrandt Peale.*

Presented by John H. Brower.

564. Portrait of Gen. Joseph Reed. (16×20.) *J. C. Hagen.*

Copy from the original by C. W. Peale.

565. Jacob's Dream. (70×51.) *Luther Terry.*

Presented by Mr. Luther Terry, in the name of the late Mrs. Eliza Hicks Rieben.

566. Portrait of Thomas J. Bryan. (25×30.)
William O. Stone.

Founder and Donor of the Bryan Collection.
Painted for the Society, 1867.

567. Portrait of Cachasunghia, Osage Warrior. (15¼×21¼.) Crayon. *St. Memin.*

568. Portrait of an Osage Warrior. (15¼×21¼.) Crayon. *St. Memin.*

569. Portrait of Payouska, Chief of the Great Osages. (15¼×21¼.) Crayon. *St. Memin.*

570. Portrait of a Chief of the Little Osages. (15¼×21¼.) Crayon. *St. Memin.*

571. Portrait of an Osage Warrior. (15¼×21¼.) Crayon. *St. Memin.*

572. Portrait of an Indian of the "Iowas of the Missouri." (15¼×21¼.) Crayon. *St. Memin.*

573. Portrait of an Indian Girl of the "Iowas of the Missouri." (15¼×21¼.) Crayon. *St. Memin.*

574. Portrait of a Delaware Indian. (15¼×21¼.) Crayon. *St. Memin*

575. Portrait of Ambrose Spencer. (25×30.) *John Wesley Jarvis.*

Presented by Marshall S. Bidwell.

576. Portrait of William W. Van Ness. (26½×33.) *John Wesley Jarvis.*

Presented by Marshall S. Bidwell.

577. Portrait of Frederic de Peyster. (29×36.) *G. Gerhard*

Painted at the request of the Society, and presented by Frederic de Peyster, 1872.

578--591. The Incas of Peru.

A collection of fourteen paintings in oil on canvass, bearing inscriptions designating the name and succession of each monarch. They are said to be the original pictures from which the portraits of the Incas were engraved for the work of Herrera—"*Historia general de los Hechos de los Castellanos*," etc., published at the beginning of the 17th century (1601-15), and reproduced in the edition by Barcia in 1726-30. This series of the Incas, as given by Herrera, differs from that of Garcilasso, in the addition of Vrco (586), who is said to have reigned only eleven days, and the omission of Yupanqui, the son of Pachacutec (587).

Presented by Frederic de Peyster.

578. Manco Capac, First Inca. (21×23.)

579. Sinchi Roca, Second Inca. (21×23.)

580. Lloqui Yupanqui, Third Inca. (21×23.)

581. Mayta Capac, Fourth Inca. (21×23.)

582. Capac Yupanqui, Fifth Inca. (21×23.)

583. Inca Roca, Sixth Inca. (21×23.)

584. Yahuar Huacac, Seventh Inca. (21×23.

585. Viracocha, Eighth Inca. (21×23.)

586. Vrco, Ninth Inca. (21×23.)

587. Pachacutec, Tenth Inca. (21×23.)

588. Tupac Yupanqui, Eleventh Inca. (21×23.)

589. Huayna Capac, Twelfth Inca. (21×23.)

590. Huascar, Thirteenth Inca. (21×23.)

591. Atahualpa, Fourteenth Inca, put to death by order of Pizarro, August 29, 1533. ($21\frac{1}{2}\times23\frac{1}{2}$.)

592. Portrait of Cinq Mars. ($31\frac{1}{2}\times41$.)
Diego Velazquez.

This picture was bought in Paris, in the year 1827, of Le Court, a miniature painter, who had it from J. B. Le Prince the well-known French artist; the latter said it was a portrait of Cinq Mars, and by Velazquez.

Bequest of T. W. C. Moore.

593. Landscape—Monks at their Devotions. ($45\frac{1}{4}\times33\frac{1}{4}$.) *Salvator Rosa.*

Bequest of T. W. C. Moore.

594. Landscape—Gypsies crossing a Brook. ($35\times27\frac{1}{4}$.) *D. Brown.*

Bought at Olmstead's sale, April, 1836, who sold it as a Morland, unaware perhaps that it was signed by Brown, who was one of his most successful imitators.

Bequest of T. W. C. Moore.

595. Landscape. (14×16.) *Matthew Withoos*

Bequest of T. W. C. Moore.

596. La Toilette. ($14\frac{1}{2}\times18$.)
Jean François De Troy

A Lady preparing for a masked Ball.

Bequest of T. W. C. Moore.

597. St. Peter after denying Christ. (6×8.)
Juan de Valdez.

Bequest of T. W. C. Moore.

598. St. John in the Desert. (6×8.)
Juan de Valdez.

Bequest of T. W. C. Moore.

NO. SUBJECTS OF PAINTINGS. ARTISTS

599. Music Party. ($28\frac{1}{2} \times 20$.)
Anthony Stevers (Palamedes)
Bequest of T. W. C. Moore.

600. Assumption of the Virgin. (24×32.)
Don Juan Carrenno de Miranda
Bought in Madrid, 1842.
Bequest of T. W. C. Moore.

601. Female Head. ($8\frac{1}{2} \times 11$.)
Sir Thomas Lawrence.
Bequest of T. W. C. Moore.

602. Doctor and Bottle. ($7\frac{1}{4} \times 9\frac{1}{2}$.) *Gerard Douw.*
This picture was purchased in Paris in 1832 during the prevalence of the cholera; it is signed by the artist with his monogram in the left-hand corner.
Bequest of T. W. C. Moore.

603. Interior—Old Man eating. ($11\frac{1}{2} \times 14\frac{1}{2}$.)
Dominick Van Tol.
Bequest of T. W. C. Moore.

604. Fruit Piece—Grapes, etc. ($19\frac{1}{2} \times 23\frac{1}{2}$.)
Nicholas Van Gelder.
Signed N. Van Gelder, 1674.
Bequest of T. W. C. Moore.

605. Fruit Piece—Strawberries, etc. ($19\frac{1}{2} \times 23\frac{1}{2}$.)
Nicholas Van Gelder
Signed N. Van Gelder, 1674.
Bequest of T. W. C. Moore.

606. Portrait of Fitz Greene Halleck. (25×30.)
Henry Inman.
This picture was painted in the year 1828 for Gen. George P. Morris.
Bequest of T. W. C. Moore.

607. Portrait of Ezra L'Hommedieu. ($27\frac{1}{2} \times 32\frac{1}{2}$). *James Earle.*
Presented by Daniel P. Ingraham.

608. Portrait of William Shaler. ($22\frac{1}{2} \times 28\frac{1}{2}$.)
U. S. Consul at Algiers and Havana.
Presented by Daniel P. Ingraham.

609. Portrait of Gilbert C. Stuart. ($3 \times 2\frac{1}{2}$.)
Anson Dickinson.
Miniature on Ivory.
Presented by S. W. and V. M. Francis.

NO. SUBJECTS OF PAINTINGS. ARTISTS

610. Portrait of Henry Clay. (25×30.)
Samuel S. Osgood.

Presented by Alice Talbot Lancey.

611. Portrait of Egbert Benson. (25×30.)
Gilbert C. Stuart.

First President of the Society. Painted from life in 1807, the original of No. 18. Presented by Robert Benson.

612. Portrait of Erastus C. Benedict. (31×39.)
William H. Powell.

Presented by Erastus C. Benedict.

613. Portrait of Robert R. Livingston. (34×45.)
John Vanderlyn.

This portrait was painted at Paris, in 1804. and presented to the American Academy of Fine Arts in New York, July 6, 1805, where it remained until that institution was dissolved.

Presented by Mrs. Thomson Livingstone.

614. Portrait of Alexander J. Dallas. (23½×29.)
John W. Jarvis.

Purchased from the American Museum Collection, 1863.
Presented by William D. Abbatt.

615. View near Sandy Hill, New York. (20½×13½.) Water-color. *William G. Wall.*

Presented by Grant Thorburn.

(New York Gallery.)

616. Portrait of Thomas De Witt, D.D. (25×30.) *William Cogswell.*

Presented by the Artist.

617. Storm at Sea. (32×19½.)

618. The Artist showing a Picture from Hamlet to his Parents. Group of Portraits, painted in 1788. (50×43.) *William Dunlap.*

Presented by Samuel C. Ellis, M.D.

619. The Bay of New York from Castle Garden. (33½×24½.)

620. Portrait of Jesse Hawley. 1836. (25×30.)
Graves S. Gilbert.

Presented by Jesse Hawley.

NO.	SUBJECTS OF PAINTINGS.	ARTISTS.

621. Portrait of a Gentleman. (26×35.)

Presented by Miss Richard.

622. Portrait of a Lady. (24×29.)

Presented by Miss Richard.

623. Portrait of a Gentleman. (25×30.)

Presented by Miss Richard.

624. Portrait of the Artist. 1841. (9×10½.) *Jeremiah Nims.*

This promising young Artist died at Kingston, Jamaica, W. I., March 6, 1842.

Presented by Mrs. Charles A. Davis.

625. Portrait of Andrew Warner. (29×36.) *George A. Baker.*

Painted for the Society, 1877.

626. Portrait of Gen. Aaron Ogden. (25×30.) *A. B. Durand.*

Governor of New Jersey, and President-General of the Society of the Cincinnati.

Painted 1834.

627. Portrait of Gulian C. Verplanck. (25×30.) *Charles C. Ingham.*

Painted about 1830.

628. Portrait of Antonio Lopez de Santa Aña. (25×30.) *Paul L'Ouvrier.*

Painted from life, about 1858.

Presented by Frederic De Peyster.

629. Vase of Flowers. (13×17.) *Mary L. Baker.*

Presented by Richard E. Mount.

630. Portrait of John A. Dix. (40×50.) *Daniel Huntington.*

Painted for the Society, 1880.

Presented by Charles O'Conor.

631. Portrait of Rev. John Rodgers, D.D. (7×9.)

Presented by Mrs. William Gerard.

632. Portrait of Jesse Hawley. (3×3½.) *Ezra Ames.*

Miniature on ivory.

Presented by Jesse Hawley.

633. Portrait of William Walton. (25×29.)

Presented by Dr. William Walton Verplanck.

THE DURR COLLECTION.

NO.	SUBJECTS OF PAINTINGS.	ARTISTS.
634.	St. Ferdinand I., King of Castile, receiving the Code de las Partidas from the Madonna. (65 × 41½.) (*Durr Collection.*)	*Murillo.*
635.	The Immaculate Conception. (24 × 32.) From the Emmet Collection. (*Durr Collection.*)	*Murillo.*
636.	**Jesus Suffering.** (19 × 24.) **Signed.** From the Emmet Collection. (*Durr Collection.*)	*J. A. Escalante.*
637.	Jesus Victorious. (19 × 24.) Signed. From the Emmet Collection. (*Durr Collection.*)	*J. A. Escalante.*
638.	St. John the Baptist. (41 × 65½.) From a collection brought from Seville, and purchased by Mr. Francis Tomes. (*Durr Collection.*)	*Velasquez.*
639.	Ecce Homo. (50 × 80.) From a Catholic church in Mexico, brought to New York about 1855. (*Durr Collection.*)	*Luis Morales.*
640.	Portrait of a Philosopher. (29 × 39.) Purchased in Philadelphia. (*Durr Collection.*)	*Spagnoletto.*
641.	Adoration of the Shepherds. (45 × 37.) Brought from Italy by Mr. W. Metcalfe. (*Durr Collection.*)	*Il Bassano.*

NO.	SUBJECTS OF PAINTINGS.	ARTISTS.

642. Martyrdom of St. Sebastian. (21 × 27.) *Tintoretto.*

(*Durr Collection.*)

643. Martyrdom of St. Lawrence. (90 × 97.) *Titian.*

This painting is signed, and shows evidences of being the first of three of this subject which Titian painted—the second, ordered by King Philip II. of Spain, remains at the Escurial; the third is in the Jesuits' Church at Venice. This composition is esteemed by such authorities as Kugler one of the most important of Titian's works.

From the collection owned by Gideon Nye, jr., who valued this picture at sixteen thousand guineas.

(*Durr Collection.*)

644. **Aretino, the Poet.** (19 × 25.) *Titian.*

The following is inscribed in French on the back of the portrait: "Collection of Alix, General-in-Chief of Westphalia.—This precious picture was found in the wagon of a vivandière, named Michau, who was killed at the battle of Marengo. After being in the possession of General Lemarois, it passed into the private cabinet of the Chevalier Denon, Director of the Musée Napoleon."

(*Durr Collection.*)

645. Assumption of the Virgin. (19½ × 40½.) *Piazetta.*

(*Durr Collection.*)

646. Italian Palace. (68½ × 47½.) *Pannini.*

From the Stone Collection.

(*Durr Collection.*)

647. Landscape. (28½ × 23½.) *Salvator Rosa.*

(*Durr Collection.*)

648. Arion and Dolphin. (60½ × 45½.) *Annibale Caracci.*

Signed.

(*Durr Collection.*)

649. Christ and the Disciples at Emmaus. (70½ × 46½.) *Paul Veronese.*

Bought in Philadelphia. The same composition, with slight variations, is in the Dresden Gallery.

(*Durr Collection.*)

650. Madonna and Child. (18 × 22½.) *Fra Bartolomeo.*

(*Durr Collection.*)

NO.	SUBJECTS OF PAINTINGS.	ARTISTS.

651. Holy Family. (7×9½.) *School of Correggio.*
(Durr Collection.)

652. Portrait of Jerome Savonarola. (22½×28½.) *Fra Bartolomeo.*
(Durr Collection.)

653. Lucretia. (22×26½.) *Venetian School, 17th Century.*
(Durr Collection.)

654. Nymphs Disarming Cupids. (14×11.) *Francesco Albano.*
(Durr Collection.)

655. Pieta. (11×15.) *Annibale Caracci.*
(Durr Collection.)

656. Bacchus and Ariadne. (51×39½.) *Titian.*
This is an old copy. The original is now in the National Gallery, London.
(Durr Collection.)

657. Palace of the Prince of Orange, in the South of France, with Portrait figures. (44×43.) *Federigo Zuccaro.*
(Durr Collection.)

658. Cattle Piece. (13×13.) *Tempesta.*
(Durr Collection.)

659. Cattle Piece. (13×13.) *Tempesta.*
(Durr Collection.)

660. Spanish Lady and Children. (67×85½.) *Velasquez.*
Purchased with Le Brun's Scenes in the Life of Alexander.
(Durr Collection.)

661–666. Scenes from the Life of Alexander the Great. (75×72.) *Charles Le Brun.*
Le Brun's larger pictures of Nos. 661, 662, 663, 665, and 666, found in the collection of Louis XIV., are in the Louvre.

661. Triumphal Entry of Alexander into Babylon.
(Durr Collection.)

NO.	SUBJECTS OF PAINTINGS.	ARTISTS.

662. Alexander and Hephestion entering the Tent of Darius.

(*Durr Collection.*)

663. Defeat of Darius at Arbela.

(*Durr Collection.*)

664. Alexander cutting the Knot of Gordius.

(*Durr Collection.*)

665. Porus brought to Alexander after his Defeat.

(*Durr Collection.*)

666. Passage of the Granicus.

(*Durr Collection.*)

667. Adoration of the Golden Calf. (70 × 49.) *Nicholas Poussin.*

Brought from Italy by James Benkard. The subject was a favorite one with Poussin.

(*Durr Collection.*)

668. Portrait of a French Gentleman. (32½ × 42.) *Hyacinthe Rigaud.*

(*Durr Collection.*)

669. Odysseus Taking Leave of Penelope. (50 × 37.) *Claude Lorraine.*

(*Durr Collection.*)

670. Evening Landscape. (39 × 31.) *Gaspar Poussin.*

(*Durr Collection.*)

671. Virgin and Child. (23½ × 36.)

Signed I. G.

(*Durr Collection.*)

672. Adoration of the Magi. (25 × 31½.) *Dutch School, 15th Century.*

(*Durr Collection.*)

673. Christ in the Prætorium. *John de Mabuse.*

Signed "IOANNES, MALBODIVS, PINCEB 1527." From the collection of Thomas Jefferson, made at Paris while United States Minister to France. Sold at Boston, July 19, 1831.

(*Durr Collection.*)

NO.	SUBJECTS OF PAINTINGS.	ARTISTS.

674. Christ Sinking Under the Cross. (13 × 18½.)
Copy from Albert Dürer.

This composition forms one of the series in the Passion, engraved by Dürer on wood.

(*Durr Collection.*)

675. Christ with the Tribute Money. (33½ × 11¾.)
Albert Dürer.

Signed A. D., dated 1525. The wings of this triptique are ornamented with the head of a Monk and of a Nun.

(*Durr Collection.*)

676. The Last Judgment. (31½ × 43½.)
Lucas Van Leyden.

(*Durr Collection.*)

677. St. Paul Preaching at Athens. (23 × 30.)
Martin Van Veen Hemskerk.

(*Durr Collection.*)

678. The Holy Night. (36 × 28.) *Karl du Jardin.*

(*Durr Collection.*)

679. Christ Before Caiaphas. (63 × 43.)
Gerard Van Herp.

Signed. This and the two following pictures, forming a series, were brought from Seville by E. Boonen Graves. From the Emmet Collection.

(*Durr Collection.*)

680. Christ Bearing the Cross. (63 × 43.)
Gerard Van Herp.

(*Durr Collection.*)

681. Christ Crowned with Thorns. (63 × 43.)
Gerard Van Herp.

(*Durr Collection.*)

682. Landing of Æneas in Italy. (60 × 40½.) *Tempesta.*

(*Durr Collection.*)

683. The Madonna. (29 × 36.) *Philip de Champagne.*

Bought by Mr. Durr at Stuttgart.

(*Durr Collection.*)

684. The Angel Gabriel. (29 × 36.)
Philip de Champagne.

Bought by Mr. Durr at Stuttgart.

(*Durr Collection.*)

NO.	SUBJECTS OF PAINTINGS.	ARTISTS.

685. Kitchen Utensils. (11 × 13.) *Barend Cornelis.*

A Dutch painter, of whose life little is known, but whose manner of handling is praised by Karel Van Mander, the art commentator of the seventeenth century, as being superior to that of his contemporaries. This picture is signed.

(*Durr Collection.*)

686. Halt at a Tavern. ($14\frac{1}{2} \times 10$). *Peter Bout.*

(*Durr Collection.*)

687. Portraits of Dr. John Bainbridge and Daughter. (38 × 50.) *Sir Peter Lely.*

Bought at the sale of the collection of Thomas Sully, December 20, 1872.

(*Durr Collection.*)

688. Portrait of a Lady. ($27 \times 33\frac{1}{2}$.) Oval. *B. Denner.*

Signed and dated 1734.

(*Durr Collection.*)

689. Portrait of a Gentleman. ($27 \times 33\frac{1}{2}$.) Oval. *B. Denner.*

Signed, and dated 1734.

(*Durr Collection.*)

690. Miracle of the Loaves and Fishes. ($43\frac{1}{2} \times 29$.) *Andreas Both.*

Purchased December, 1865, from the collection of Joseph M. Meert de Domberg.

(*Durr Collection.*)

691. Moses Striking the Rock. ($43\frac{1}{2} \times 29$.) *Andreas Both.*

In this picture almost every position of the human body is represented. It is from the collection of Joseph M. Meert de Domberg.

(*Durr Collection.*)

692. Still Life. ($41 \times 47\frac{1}{2}$.) *Van Westhofen.*

(*Durr Collection.*)

693. Portrait of a Gentleman. (15 × 19.) *School of Van Dyck.*

(*Durr Collection.*)

694. Landscape with Spanish Figures. ($53\frac{1}{2} \times 49\frac{1}{2}$.) *Lucas Vanuden.*

(*Durr Collection.*)

NO.	SUBJECTS OF PAINTINGS.	ARTISTS.

695. Landscape, with Cattle. (48 × 37½.)
John H. Roos.

This and the following picture were purchased in Bavaria by Mr. Keller.

(*Durr Collection.*)

696. Landscape, with Cattle. (48 × 37½.)
John H. Roos.

(*Durr Collection.*)

697. Crossing the River. (23 × 16½.)
Solomon Ruysdael.

(*Durr Collection.*)

698. Passage of the Red Sea. (32 × 25.)
Francis Francken, the Elder.

Brought by Mr. Forbes from Sicily.

(*Durr Collection.*)

699. The Crucifixion. (26 × 20.)
Francis Francken, the Elder.

From the collection of John G. Boker.

(*Durr Collection.*)

700. Landscape with Figures. (40 × 24½.)
D. Hagelstein.

A pupil of A. Elzheimer, figures by C. Poelemburg. Signed and dated 1630.

(*Durr Collection.*)

701. Game. (47 × 36½.) *J. B. Weenix.*

(*Durr Collection.*)

702. The Riverside. (21 × 14½.)
Jan Van Hughtenburg.

(*Durr Collection.*)

703. Marine. (22 × 17½.) *L. Backhuysen.*

(*Durr Collection.*)

704. Expulsion of Adam and Eve. (94 × 69.)
A. Bloemaert.

(*Durr Collection.*)

705. Mother and Child. (27½ × 35.) *Jan Victoor.*

Purchased February, 1870, at the sale of the collection of Thomas Thompson.

(*Durr Collection.*)

NO. SUBJECTS OF PAINTINGS. ARTISTS.

706. Landscape. (9 × 11.) *Anthony Waterloo.*

(*Durr Collection.*)

707. Reptiles, Birds, and Insects. (29 × 38½.) *Otho Marcellis.*

Signed and dated, 1667. From the collection of Gideon Nye, Jr.

(*Durr Collection.*)

708. The Flute Player. (41 × 33.) *James Vanloo.*

Purchased February, 1870, from the collection of Thomas Thompson.

(*Durr Collection.*)

709. The Bean King. (36 × 29.) *John Molinaer.*

Signed.

(*Durr Collection.*)

710. The Rhinefall at Schaffhouse. (18½ × 13½.)

Signed A. K., 1669.

(*Durr Collection.*)

711. Moonlight Landscape. (17 × 15.) *Claude Joseph Vernet.*

(*Durr Collection.*)

712. Kitchen Utensils. (10 × 11.) *William Kalf.*

(*Durr Collection.*)

713. Portrait of a Lady. (23 × 30.) *German School.*

(*Durr Collection.*)

714. The Music Lesson—Effect of Candle-light. (37½ × 27½.) *Gerard Honthorst.*

(*Durr Collection.*)

715. Portrait of Lucretia Van der Meulen. (28 × 34½.) *John Van Ravesteyn.*

Signed.

(*Durr Collection.*)

716. Sealing the Letter—Effect of Candle-light. (37½ × 27½.) *Gerard Honthorst.*

(*Durr Collection.*)

717. Portrait of a Lady. (23 × 29.) *John de Baan.*

(*Durr Collection.*)

NO.	SUBJECTS OF PAINTINGS.	ARTISTS.

718. Winter Landscape. (22 × 17½.)

Signed, J. V. E. From the Beckett Collection, Philadelphia.

(*Durr Collection.*)

719. Hunters Resting. (14½ × 17½.) *John Miel.*

(*Durr Collection.*)

720. Landscape. (22 × 19.) *John Wynants.*

From the Beckett Collection, Philadelphia.

(*Durr Collection.*)

721. Stag Hunt. (24 × 19.) *Gerard Van Battem.*

Signed.

(*Durr Collection.*)

722. Evening Landscape. (32½ × 23½.)
Minderhout Hobbema.

Signed. Purchased from Mr. Joseph Vollmering.

(*Durr Collection.*)

723. Farm House with Cattle. (34½ × 22.)
Albert Cuyp.

(*Durr Collection.*)

724. Evening Landscape. (32½ × 22½.)
A. Verboom.

Signed.

(*Durr Collection.*)

725. The Happy Burgher. (8 × 9.) *Ary de Voys.*

(*Durr Collection.*)

726. Huntsman Feeding his Dogs. (22 × 15½.)
Cornelis Saftleven.

(*Durr Collection.*)

727. Landscape. (21 × 16.) *Adam Pynaker.*

(*Durr Collection.*)

728. Interior of a Dutch Tavern. (21 × 15.)
Egbert van Hemskerk, the Younger.

(*Durr Collection.*)

729. Interior.—Dutch Kitchen. (18½ × 25.)
Q. Brekelenkamp.

Signed.

(*Durr Collection.*)

NO.	SUBJECTS OF PAINTINGS.	ARTISTS.

730. Arrival of the Dutch Fleet at Amsterdam. (26×16½.) *W. van de Velde, the Younger.*
(*Durr Collection.*)

731. Women Bathing. (11½×8½.) *Daniel Vertangen.*
(*Durr Collection.*)

732. The Flight into Egypt. (4½×5½.) *Dutch School, 16th Century.*
(*Durr Collection.*)

733. Starting for the Pasture. (21½×17½.) *David Teniers, the Younger.*
(*Durr Collection.*)

734. Dutch Interior.—Washerwomen. (28×21.) *Henry M. Rokes.*
(*Durr Collection.*)

735. Interior of a Church. (33×26.) *Anthony de Lorme.*
A Dutch painter of architecture, about 1660. Figures by A. VAN DE VELDE. The picture is signed. From the Emmet Collection.
(*Durr Collection.*)

736. Combat of Cavalry. (33½×20½.) *Rembrandt.*
From the collection of Gideon Nye, Jr. Signed.
(*Durr Collection.*)

737. The Deluge. (9×7.) *Daniel Vertangen.*
From the Beckett Collection, Philadelphia.
(*Durr Collection.*)

738. Tavern Interior. (12×8½.) *Isaac Van Ostade.*
(*Durr Collection.*)

739–743. Allegorical Representation of the Five Senses. (12×8.) *Adrian Van Ostade.*
From the Beckett Collection, Philadelphia. The subject was a favorite one with the artist. A repetition of No. 739 will be found in No. 548 of this catalogue.

739. Sight.
(*Durr Collection.*)

740. Hearing.
(*Durr Collection.*)

NO.	SUBJECTS OF PAINTINGS.	ARTISTS.

741. Taste.

(*Durr Collection.*)

742. Touch.

(*Durr Collection.*)

743. Smell.

(*Durr Collection.*)

744. Mars and Venus. (19 × 14.) *J. Rottenhamer.*

The background is painted by JOHN BREUGHEL. This painting has been engraved by J. D. Herz.

(*Durr Collection.*)

745. Entombment of Christ. (36 × 28½.) *Rubens.*

Old copy. Original in the Vienna Gallery. From the Thompson Collection, February, 1870.

(*Durr Collection.*)

746. Hunting Party. (41 × 28½.)
Simon van der Does.

(*Durr Collection.*)

747. Frederick I., Emperor of Germany, surnamed "Barbarossa." (19 × 36½.)
Lucas Cranach.

(*Durr Collection.*)

748. Vegetable Vender. (24½ × 18.) *John Doncker.*

Signed, J. DONCK, 1630.

(*Durr Collection.*)

749. Tavern Scene. (23 × 19½.)
John Horremans, the Elder.

(*Durr Collection.*)

750. Tavern Scene. (23 × 19½.)
John Horremans, the Elder.

(*Durr Collection.*)

751. Italian Landscape. (22 × 15.)
J. F. van Bloemen.

(*Durr Collection.*)

752. Birds and Fish. (22 × 16½.) *Albert Flamen.*

(*Durr Collection.*)

NO.	SUBJECTS OF PAINTINGS.	ARTISTS.

753. **Storm at Sea.** (29½ × 19.) *Bonaventura Peters.*
(*Durr Collection.*)

754. A Dutch Interior.—Beggars Carousing.
(27½ × 21.) *Adrian Brower.*
Signed. From the collection of Joseph M. Meert de Domberg.
(*Durr Collection.*)

755. Seaport. (25½ × 20½.) *L. Backhuysen.*
(*Durr Collection.*)

756. A Sea Fight. (28 × 21.) *John Lingelbach.*
(*Durr Collection.*)

757. Rendezvous of Smugglers. (25 × 20.)
John van Geel.
(*Durr Collection.*)

758. Tavern Interior. (16½ × 20.) *Peter van der Elst.*
(*Durr Collection.*)

759. Burning of a Cottage at Night.
(15 × 16½.) *Egbert vander Poel.*
(*Durr Collection.*)

760. Burning of a Cottage at Night. (19 × 14½.)
Egbert vander Poel.
(*Durr Collection.*)

761. Landscape with Figures and Cattle. (22 × 15.)
Nicholas Berghem.
(*Durr Collection.*)

762. Fruit Piece. (21 × 15½.) *Albert Cuyp.*
(*Durr Collection.*)

763. Dutch Windmill. (16 × 13½.)
John vander Meer.
Signed and dated 1693. From the Stone Collection.
(*Durr Collection.*)

764. Card Players. (17½ × 13½.) *Leonard de France.*
From the Beckett Collection, Philadelphia.
(*Durr Collection.*)

765. Landscape with Cattle. (15½ × 11½.)
Karl du Jardin.
(*Durr Collection.*)

NO.	SUBJECTS OF PAINTINGS.	ARTISTS

766. Flowers. (28 × 33.) *Simon Verelst.*

(*Durr Collection.*)

767. Playing the Bagpipe. (8 × 9½.) *John Tilius.*

(*Durr Collection.*)

768. Landscape with Figures. (14 × 12.) *Philip Wouvermans.*

From the Beckett Collection, Philadelphia.

(*Durr Collection.*)

769. The Pedler. (8 × 9½.)

From the Beckett Collection, Philadelphia.

(*Durr Collection.*)

770. Chateau and Park. (12 × 9½.) *John vander Heyden.*

(*Durr Collection.*)

771. Samson and Delilah. (33½ × 25.) *Van Dyck.*

The finished picture of this sketch is in the Belvidere Gallery, Vienna.

(*Durr Collection.*)

772. Historical Subject. (40 × 34.) *G. van den Eckhout.*

Signed, "P. Isaacksen, Invent'. G. v. Eckhout, pingsit. A.D. 1670."

(*Durr Collection.*)

773. Interior of a Church. (20 × 23.) *Emanuel de Witt.*

(*Durr Collection.*)

774. Dutch Interior—Effect of Candle-light. (28½ × 22.) *David Ryckaert.*

(*Durr Collection.*)

775. The Magi Going to Bethlehem. (41½ × 30½.) *Leonard Bramer.*

(*Durr Collection.*)

776. Musical Party. (10½ × 11.) *Matthew Van Helmont.*

Signed.

(*Durr Collection.*)

NO. SUBJECTS OF PAINTINGS. ARTISTS.

777. Farm-yard—Peasants Playing Cards. (22 × 18.) *Karl du Jardin.*

Signed, and dated 1667.
(*Durr Collection.*)

778. Landscape. (31 × 26.) *John Wynants.*

Signed.
(*Durr Collection.*)

779. Landscape with Sheep and Figures. (24 × 18.) *B. P. Ommeganck*

(*Durr Collection.*)

780. The Pasture-field. (19 × 14½.) *Jan Kobell.*

(*Durr Collection.*)

781. Kitchen Interior. (9½ × 12.) *H. Van Hove.*

(*Durr Collection.*)

782. Family Group. (14 × 18.) *F. G. Waldmüller.*

(*Durr Collection.*)

783. View on the Moselle River. (18 × 15½.) *Bernard C. Koekkoek.*

(*Durr Collection.*)

784. Halt at the Tavern. (24 × 19.) *Baron Henry Leys.*

(*Durr Collection.*)

785. Wayside Hospitality. (9½ × 7½.) *Fritz Franz.*

(*Durr Collection.*)

786. Evening Landscape—Sunset. (17 × 11.)

(*Durr Collection.*)

787. Germania. (108 × 90.) *Christian Köhler.*

The struggle of the German people in the year 1848 gave rise to this allegorical composition. Germania, the Goddess of Germany, awakened from her slumber on a bear's skin by Justice and Liberty, seizes the national crown and sword, and drives away the demons of Despotism and Discord. This picture was finished in 1849, when it was purchased by Mr. John G. Boker, and brought by him to New York, where for many years it was exhibited in the Düsseldorf Gallery.

(*Durr Collection.*)

NO.	SUBJECTS OF PAINTINGS.	ARTISTS.

796. Portrait of John Payne. (25×30.)
Thomas G. Wainewright.

The two preceding portraits, of father and son, celebrated London booksellers, were obtained from Mr. J. T. Payne, grandson, by Mr. F. S. Ellis, of London, and by him presented to the Society, 1883.

797. Portrait of a Lady. (34×46.)

Presented by Frederic de Peyster.

798. Portrait of a Gentleman. (34×46.)

This and the preceding picture came from Castleton, Staten Island, N. Y., the former residence of the Colonial Governor, Colonel Thomas Dongan. They are portraits of members of the Dongan family, and were purchased from the collection of the Hon. Caleb Lyon, January, 1882.

Presented by Frederic de Peyster.

799. Portrait of Nicholas P. Trist. 1852. (25×30.)
Robert M. Pratt.

Presented, 1884, by Miss Eugenia C. Pratt.

800. Portrait of Richard Hildreth. 1858. (25×30.)
Robert M. Pratt.

Presented, 1884, by Miss Eugenia C. Pratt.

801. Portrait of N. P. Willis. (28×36.)

802. Portrait of Roger Strong. (10×28½.)
John Vanderlyn.

Presented by Miss Frances E. Mankin, 1885.

803. Portrait of Robert Benson. (24×30.)
John Trumbull.

Painted, 1804, when the subject was in his 65th year.
Bequest of Robert Benson, Jr., 1883.

804. Portrait of Henry Benson. (25×30.)
John Vanderlyn.

Painted, 1823, when the subject was 80 years of age.
Bequest of Robert Benson, Jr., 1883.

805. Portrait of Augustus Schell. (22×27.)
Eastman Johnson.

President of the Society, 1872, 1883–84. Painted 1885.
Presented by Mrs. Anna Schell.

NO.	SUBJECTS OF PAINTINGS.	ARTISTS.

806. Portrait of Benjamin H. Field. (29×36.)
Daniel Huntington.

President of the Society, 1885-86. Painted 1875.
Bequest of Mrs. Catharine M. Van Cortlandt Field.

807. Shandaken Range, Kingston, N. Y. (16¼×21½.)
A. B. Durand.

(*Durr Collection.*)

808. Trees by the Brookside, Kingston, N. Y. (16½×21.)
A. B. Durand.

(*Durr Collection.*)

809. Study at Marbletown, N. Y. (16¾×21.)
A. B. Durand.

(*Durr Collection.*)

810. Group of Trees. (17½×23¼.)
A. B. Durand.

(*Durr Collection.*)

811. Return of the 69th Regiment, N. Y. S. M., from the Seat of War. (140×87.) *Louis Lang.*

This regiment returned to the city of New York, on the morning of the 27th of July, 1861, after three months' service in the South, when it received a popular ovation, which the artist has faithfully depicted. The picture represents the troops turning into Broadway from Battery Place, where they had landed. The faces are mainly studies from life.

Presented by the artist, 1886.

812. Portrait of John Lawrance. (Miniature.)
John Trumbull.

Judge-Advocate-General, War of the Revolution, Member of Congress, and U. S. Senator from New York, Judge U.S. District Court.

Painted at Philadelphia, 1792.

Presented by J. L. and G. C. McWhorter, 1886.

SCULPTURE.

---

1. **Ruth.** *Henry K. Brown*

"The artist has chosen the moment in which Ruth is addressed by Boaz as she stands among the gleaners. He quoted the lines of Keats in the song of the Nightingale—

'Perchance the self-same song hath found a path
To the sad heart of Ruth, when, sick for home,
She stood in tears amid the alien corn.'

She is not in tears; but her aspect is that of one who listens in sadness; her eyes are cast down, and her thoughts are of the home of her youth in the land of Moab. Over her left arm hangs a handful of the ears of wheat which she has gathered from the ground, and her right rests on the drapery about her bosom. Nothing can be more graceful than her attitude, or more expressive of melancholy sweetness and modesty than her physiognomy."—*Extract of a letter by Mr W. C. Bryant, dated Rome*, 1845.

This statue was purchased by Miss Hicks, of New York, and presented to the New York Gallery of Fine Arts.

2 Group of Boy and Dog; or, *Chi Vinci, mangia.* *Henry K. Brown*

This playful group was presented to the New York Gallery, by C. M. Leupp, Esq. The boy has left his bowl of milk upon the floor, and the dog is endeavoring to take advantage of his negligence, by appropriating the contents to himself, against which the boy stoutly protests. They are so equally matched in strength, that the struggle is of doubtful issue, and therefore the artist calls it, "*Chi vinci, mangia*," or, who wins, eats.

No.	SUBJECTS.	ARTISTS

3. The Triumphal March of the Republic. *A. Ottin*

Bas-relief in plaster. Executed by M. Ottin, by order of the Government of the French Republic, in 1848. It was designed to be completed in marble for the front of the tribune in the Chamber of Deputies.

Presented by the artist, 1857.

4. Bust of J. M. White. *In marble.*
Horatio Greenough.

Presented by Mrs. Charles A. Davis.

5. A Bacchante. *Nicolas Coustou.*

(*Bryan Collection.*)

6. Bust of Christopher Columbus. *In marble.*
John Gott.

Presented by John E. Williams.

7. Bust of John Quincy Adams. *In marble.*
Horatio Greenough.

Presented by Augustus H. Ward.

8. Bust of William Cullen Bryant. *In marble.*
Henry K. Brown.

Legacy of Charles M. Leupp.

9. Bust of Washington Allston. *In marble.*
E. A. Brackett.

Legacy of Charles M. Leupp.

10. Bust of Washington Irving. *In marble.*
E. D. Palmer.

Presented by Mrs. Anna T. E. Kirtland.

11. Bust of George Washington. *J. A. Houdon.*

Presented by David Hosack.

12. Bust of John Marshall.

13. Bust of George Clinton. *Giuseppe Ceracchi.*

14 Bust of Benjamin Franklin.
Jean Antoine Houdon.

Presented by David Hosack.

NO	SUBJECTS.	ARTISTS.
15.	Bust of Alexander Hamilton. From the original by Ceracchi, N. Y. Eve. Post, Sept. 18, 1804. Presented by the Artist.	*John Dixey.*
16.	Bust of John Jay.	*Giuseppe Ceracchi.*
17.	Bust of Benjamin West. Presented by Luther Bradish.	*Francis Chantrey.*
18.	Bust of Thomas Paine. Presented by the Artist.	*John Wesley Jarvis.*
19.	Bust of Peter Augustus Jay. Presented by Henry E. Pierrepont.	*Robert E. Launitz.*
20.	Bust of Joel Barlow.	*Jean Antoine Houdon.*
21.	Bust of James Kent. Presented by John Jay.	*Shobal V. Clevenger.*
22.	Bust of John Quincy Adams.	
23.	Bust of Oliver Wolcott.	*Shobal V. Clevenger*
24.	Bust of William Henry Harrison. Presented by Benjamin R. Winthrop.	*Shobal V. Clevenger.*
25.	Bust of De Witt Clinton. Presented by John Pintard.	
26.	Bust of Daniel Webster.	
27.	Bust of Henry Clay. Presented by Samuel Verplanck.	*Shobal V. Clevenger.*
28.	Bust of David Hosack. Presented by John W. Francis, M.D.	*John H. I. Browere.*
29.	Bust of John Wakefield Francis, M. D. Presented by S. W. Francis, M. D.	
30.	Bust of Lord Nelson. Presented by Prior and Dunning.	

NO.	SUBJECTS OF PAINTINGS.	ARTISTS.

788. The Wood Road. (34 × 28.) *P. Barbiers.*

Signed.

(Durr Collection.)

789. The Lute Player. (25 × 30.)

Gilbert Stewart Newton.

(Durr Collection.)

790. Group of Fishermen on the Seashore. (60 × 43½.)

Albert Cuyp.

Signed.

(Durr Collection.)

791. The Three Marys. (27 × 36.) *Bernardino Luini.*

(Durr Collection.)

792. Portrait of Cornelius Steenwyck. (24½ × 13½.)

Jan Van Goosen.

Steenwyck was prominent in the early annals of New York as Burgomaster, etc., under the Dutch, and Member of the Assembly, Alderman, Member of the Council, and Mayor under the English rule. This picture is supposed to have been painted at Haarlem, Holland, 1667–68, at which time Steenwyck was visiting his sister, the wife of the artist Van Goosen. It remained for more than a century in the family of Colonel Anthony White, from one of whose descendants—Miss Isabella J. Evans, of New Brunswick, N. J.—it came into the possession of the Society in December, 1882.

The portrait is surmounted by the arms of Steenwyck, and below it is a view of the city of New Amsterdam, from a sketch made about 1656. The head of Steenwyck, No. 148 of this Catalogue, seems to have been copied from this picture.

793. The Lover's Present. (12 × 15.) *S. Freudenberger.*

Water-color of a lady receiving a present of a spaniel dog. Signed and dated Paris, 1770.

(Bryan Collection.)

794. Bacchante and Satyr. (59 × 44.)

John Vanderlyn.

From the original by ANNIBALE CARACCI in the Pitti Palace.

795. Portrait of Thomas Payne. (23 × 29.)

G. Vander Puyl.

Original of the portrait engraved for Dibdin's Decameron.

No.	SUBJECTS.	ARTISTS
31	Bust of Simon Bolivar.	*Petrus Tener.*
	Presented by Alexander H. Stevens, M. D.	
32.	Bust of Joseph Hume.	*Bonomi.*
	Presented by James B. Murray.	
33.	Bust of Edward Everett.	*Shobal V. Clevenger.*
34.	Bust of Thomas C. Brownell, D. D.	*C. B. Ives.*
	Presented by G. W. Burnham.	
35.	Bust of Elisha Kent Kane, M. D.	*Peter Reniers.*
	Presented by Rev. Francis L. Hawks, D. D.	
36.	Bust of Sir Walter Scott.	
	Presented by Samuel W. Francis, M. D.	
37.	Bust of William H. Seward.	
	Presented by Charles A. Stetson.	
38.	Bust of Philip Hone.	*Shobal V. Clevenger*
	Presented by James Herring.	
39.	Bust of John Watts.	*Thomas Coffee.*
	From the original by Ball Hughes. Presented by J. Watts De Peyster.	
40.	Bust of Abraham Lincoln.	*T. D. Jones.*
	Presented by H. L. Stuart.	
41.	Bust of D. J. Macgowan.	*Clark Mills.*
42.	Medallion of Washington. *In bronze.*	*Alfred W. Jones.*
	Presented by the Artist.	
43.	Bust of Hugh Williamson, M.D. (1816.)	*William I. Coffee.*
44.	Bust of Thomas Jefferson.	*Jean Antoine Houdon.*
	Presented by Mrs. Laura Wolcott Gibbs.	
45.	Bust of Benjamin Silliman.	*C. B. Ives*

NO.	SUBJECTS	ARTISTS

46. Bust of Lamartine. *In marble.* (1854.) *A. S. Adam-Salomon.*

Presented by the family of the late Colonel Washington A. Bartlett, through George L. Ditson, M.D.

47. Medallion of Francis L. Hawks, D.D. *In marble.* *David Richards.*

Presented by William Niblo.

48. Medallion of Nathaniel Hawthorne. *Edward J. Kuntze*

Presented by the Artist.

49. Bust of William Pitt.

Published Jan., 1800, by R. Shout, Holborn, London.
Presented by George Gibbs.

50. Bust of Charles James Fox.

Published by R. Shout, Holborn.
Presented by George Gibbs.

51. Bust of James R. Wood, M.D.

Presented by Samuel W. Francis, M.D.

52. Bust of William H. Prescott. *Thomas Ball.*

Presented by William A. Greene.

53. Bust of Thaddeus Kosciusko. *Eggenschwiler.*

54. The Indian. *Thomas Crawford.*

This sculpture is a repetition of the well known figure in *The Progress of Civilization in America*, a group executed by order of the Government for the Capitol extension at Washington.

"Resting on a low mound is seated the Indian chief, a nude figure excellently modeled. His head, crowned with tufted feathers, rests sadly upon his hand, the weary chase of life is over, he is dying—the Great Spirit waits to conduct him to the far off hunting-grounds, that dreamy land where souls repose in boundless prairies. His tribe has disappeared, he is left alone, the solitary offshoot of a mighty race; already the axe of the backwoodsman disturbs his last hours; civilization, and art, and agriculture—all mysteries to him incomprehensible—have desecrated his home, and the dark shadows of the past gather him into their bosom!"—*London Art Journal.*

Purchased from the family of the Artist, and presented by Frederic de Peyster, President of the Society, April 6, 1875.

55. Bust of Philip Hone. *John H. I. Browere.*

Presented by Mrs. John Anthon.

NO.	SUBJECTS.	ARTISTS

56. Bust of William Shakspeare.

A cast from the Bust in Stratford Church, from the collection of George Daniel.

Presented by George Adlard.

57. Statue of William Pitt. *In marble.*
Joseph Wilton.

Erected by the Colony of New York, Sept. 7, 1770, at the intersection of Wall and William streets. It was mutilated by the British soldiers soon after their occupation of New York City in 1776.

Presented by Simon F. Mackie.

58. Bust of Francis L. Hawks, D. D. *In marble.*
David Richards.

Presented by the Vestry of the Church of the Holy Saviour, N. Y., 1877.

59. Bust of William Beach Lawrence. (1877.)
In marble. *F. A. T. Dunbar.*

Presented by Mr. Isaac Lawrence, Jan. 3, 1882.

60. Bust of Louis Durr.
In Bronze. *Henry Baerer.*

Founder of the Durr Collection.

Presented by the Executors of his Estate.

61. Achilles and Penthesilea. *Group in Marble.*
G. M. Benzoni.

Presented by the children of the late Charles H. Russell, 1886.

62. Bust of Samuel Osgood, D.D. (1869.)
Franklin Simmons.

Presented by Mrs. Ellen H. Osgood, 1887.

THE LENOX COLLECTION OF NINEVEH SCULPTURES.

PRESENTED BY JAMES LENOX, ESQ.

1. Winged figure with triple horns standing with a fir cone in one hand, in the other a basket ornamented with a bas-relief of two kings beside a sacred tree.

2. Two small winged figures kneeling beside two sacred trees—underneath twenty lines of inscription. This slab is placed over the following.

3. Two small eagle-headed human figures with offerings —a tree between them, and another behind one of the figures.

4 and 5. (Subject extending over two adjoining slabs.) In the centre a sacred tree; on either side a winged figure standing each with double horns, and each presenting the mystic firecone and basket —behind one of them another sacred tree. The sandals retain remains of black and red paint.

6. Eagle-headed human figure with offerings before a sacred tree.

7. The sacred tree. This is connected with the preceding.

8. Winged figure with triple horns, with the usual offerings, standing between two sacred trees.

9. Similar figure reversed.

10. Winged figure standing with a mystic basket in one hand, the other hand open.

11. Similar figure reversed.

12. Winged figure standing, before him a king with a patera in one hand and a bow in the other, each of which exhibits some unusual ornamentation.

13. Eagle-headed human figure, (supposed Nisroch,) standing with mystic offerings between two sacred trees.

The following described Pictures were STOLEN from the BRYAN COLLECTION before it was received by the Society.

Cupid discharging an Arrow. *In the style of Correggio.*

Cupid after the discharge of the Arrow—with finger raised constraining silence. *In the style of Correggio.*

Adoration of the Magi. *Leonard Bramer.*

The Virgin, with the infant Christ and Joseph, sits in front of a ruined building. Around them the Magi are grouped in adoration. The distribution of the light in this little picture is truly grand, and the color is rich and harmonious. The influence of Rembrandt is apparent in every touch.

Vision of St. Louis. *Anthony Van Dyck.*

The sainted King starts from a canopied couch to gaze upon the apparition of Pope GREGORY IV., who appears before him, cloud-borne, and surrounded by angels. In the background is a sentinel. This little picture is noble in style and harmonious in color. The action of the figures is remarkably free and vigorous.

A Lace-Worker. *Peter De Hooghe.*

A young woman sits by an open window, with her hands resting upon the cushion on which is her work. The light falls in a broad mass upon one side of her face and figure, while the other is in the half-shadow of reflected light. This little sketch, so unobtrusive in subject and treatment, will impress the close observer with a sense of great power and thorough knowledge—knowledge which is content to know without seeming learned.

Miniature Portrait. *Balthazar Denner.*

An old man, wearing a cap, and a breastplate over a rich doublet. This head is painted with an elaborateness of detail worthy of Gerard Douw, while at the same time it is modelled with a free and learned hand.

(*Collection of General Count Turenne.*)

INDEX.

www.ingramcontent.com/pod-product-compliance
Lightning Source LLC
Chambersburg PA
CBHW020547270326
41927CB00006B/757
9783743304413